Theatre for Young Audiences
a critical handbook

Theatre for Young Audiences
a critical handbook

edited by Tom Maguire and
Karian Schuitema

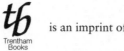 is an imprint of

UCL Institute of Education Press
20 Bedford Way
London
WC1H 0AL

First published 2012

British Library Cataloguing-in-Publication Data
A catalogue record for this book is available from the British Library

ISBN 978-1-85856-501-9

Printed and bound by CPI Group (UK) Ltd, Croydon, CR0 4YY

Contents

Foreword

David Wood

Theatre for young audiences is an art form. There, I have said it. Theatre for children and young people is an art form. Full stop. Since 1967, when I wrote my first play for children, I have always qualified that statement with, 'I believe that ...' or, 'it may sound pretentious, but in my opinion ...' This book has at last given me the confidence to state firmly that, along with opera, ballet and mime, children's theatre and theatre created specifically for teenagers is an art form in its own right, not just a junior version of adult or 'real' theatre. At last here is a book that takes our work seriously, that sees it as worthy of academic interest, study and comment; a book that recognises that an audience of children and young people brings a unique set of challenges to playwrights, actors, directors and designers, who develop through practice ways of working that may employ the techniques of adult theatre, but also necessitate a specific understanding of how the young audience reacts *en masse*.

The contributors to this book acknowledge how difficult it is to create theatre for children and young people, to hold their attention and trigger their imaginations. They do not relegate specialist children's theatre practitioners to the second division. They do not assume that they are cutting their teeth, aiming to eventually climb the ladder towards the goal of doing grown-up theatre. For too long this has been the accepted perception of most children's arts practitioners. As Philip Pullman memorably commented, it is like assuming paediatric hospital consultants are cutting their teeth on little people before graduating to the more arduous, and more prestigious, treatment of big people.

No, we children's theatre practitioners do it because we want to, because we relish the challenge and responsibility of working for and with unseasoned, often first-time, theatregoers. A positive reaction from them gives us a great buzz. And hopefully we encourage some of them to grow up enjoying theatre. But such investment in the future is not our spur: we want to give young audiences exciting theatre NOW, for its own sake, rather than do it to create tomorrow's adult audiences. And we do not believe it is good enough to say children and teenagers do not need their own theatre, that early exposure to Shakespeare or pantomime or a big musical will do the job.

We welcome the fact that academics are now helping to raise the profile and status of our work by analysing its ingredients, its variety and its effects. Having accepted that theatre for young audiences is a worthy subject of study, we need academics to trace its history as a mode of entertainment and education, and its contribution to the life of a civilised society, both here in the UK and internationally. Hopefully this book will inspire our universities and theatre training establishments to encourage more academics and teachers to focus on the work and celebrate how it has developed so success-fully, and against all the odds, since Peter Pan flew into the Darlings' nursery in 1904.

My own involvement in theatre for children started in the 1960s. I had no sense of being part of a growing movement, although my first job was in a Theatre In Education team. From its beginnings at the Belgrade Theatre, Coventry, TIE subsequently spread around the country, with teams of actor/ teachers performing in schools. Their 'projects', with an overtly educational theme and purpose, contrasted with the earlier work of pioneers like Bertha Waddell and her Scottish Children's Theatre, Caryl Jenner who – pre-Unicorn Theatre – toured children's plays to schools and village halls, and Nicholas Stuart Gray, whose fairytale adaptations played seasons in London. Brian Way created plays involving the participation of children alongside professional actors, and Peter Slade developed the idea of drama as a creative tool in the classroom. Working in theatre buildings was, to me, more exciting than work-ing in schools, even though I much enjoyed my TIE involvement and always appreciated its value. But I loved the idea of the children coming to the theatre and experiencing the magic we could more easily create there than in the classroom. So my plays were performed in theatres and on tour, and were aimed at both school parties and families.

The schism that developed between TIE and children's theatre has never been fully studied. Hopefully this book may lead to such an enterprise. In simple terms, the TIE lobby disliked theatres as middle-class institutions and thought children's theatre was whimsical and trivial. The children's theatre folk felt TIE was too educational and lacking in entertainment value. Eventually, in my view, elements of both disciplines successfully merged and plays began to be produced that combined the integrity and thoughtfulness of TIE with the theatre magic and entertainment value of children's theatre. The best of both.

Sadly, TIE declined, mainly thanks to the policies of Mrs Thatcher, which led to local educational authorities withdrawing funding. Many TIE practitioners adapted to the new situation. And many children's theatre practitioners grew to use TIE techniques. And, in the last twenty years, we have seen a welcome explosion of companies creating work specifically for young audiences, both commercial and subsidised, producing exciting work that plays in schools, studio spaces, theatres and the open air.

In spite of ongoing funding problems, caused partly by the necessary low seat price, theatre for young audiences has at last become an integral part of many theatres' programming. They sometimes produce their own work, they sometimes welcome touring products. Since I began, and from the time I ran my company Whirligig Theatre (1979-2004), the landscape has changed hugely and positively. It has been a joy, and in some ways a vindication, to witness this growth. Now we have splendid specialist companies, like Oily Cart, who perform for children and young people with all kinds of disability. And an increasing number of companies target the under-5s with imaginative, colourful and inspiring work. All this activity is worthy of academic evaluation and research.

This book may also lead to academic enquiry into specific ingredients of theatre for young audiences. For example, the role of audience participation, the importance of physical theatre techniques such as choreography and circus skills, the use of music, and the role of the designer and the visual power of costume, settings and lighting. Another useful investigation might be made into the subject of adaptation. Box office demands have long encouraged the need for a familiar title. Adaptations of well-known stories, fairytales, films and television programmes are rife: I have done several myself. Is this healthy? Does it detract from the development of new ideas and subject matter? And last, but not least, how can we best evaluate the quality of a child's experience when watching or taking part in theatre?

Thank you, Karian and Tom, for creating this book, and thank you, contributors, for agreeing that theatre for young audiences is an art form. There, I've said it again.

David Wood OBE ('the national children's dramatist' – *The Times*)
November 2011

1
Introduction
Tom Maguire and Karian Schuitema

Introduction

Theatre for Young Audiences (TYA) in the UK is an area full of contrasts and negotiations. On the one hand, there are companies that provide theatre specifically for children and young people, all of which enrich the field with their own artistic visions and approaches towards entertainment and art for the young. On the other hand, there are the dominant drivers within the area of TYA who are external to the artistic process: funding bodies, venue managers and programmers, as well as those who bring children to the theatre (parents, carers and educators). All exert an influence manifest in the constant need to justify and validate productions and agendas.

This volume of essays adds substance to the understanding of this area by encouraging and reflecting upon the growing interest in the topic and illustrating the emergence of a wide range of practices and perspectives. It is comprised of new and original work by contributors who are pioneers in the fledgling but steadily growing field of studies in TYA in the UK.

History

The making of theatre specifically targeting young audiences in the United Kingdom has a long and varied history. Stuart Bennett notes some examples of early 'touring companies with dramatisations of folk and fairy tales' in the late nineteenth and early twentieth century (2005:12). Nonetheless, the development of theatre for the child is rooted in very early, arguably foundational, plays such as *Katawampus* (1901), *Peter Pan* (1904) and *Where the Rainbow Ends* (1911). In his foreword to this volume David Wood draws attention to Bertha Waddell's Scottish Children's Theatre, founded in 1927, noting elsewhere the important premiere in 1929 of *Toad of Toad Hall*, adapted by AA Milne from Kenneth Grahame's *Wind in The Willows* (Wood and Grant, 1997:9).

These examples notwithstanding, it is easy to agree with Bennett's argument that TYA developed as a distinct form of professional theatre in the UK in the latter half of the twentieth century. He does an invaluable job of identifying the key pioneers in the field: Caryl Jenner and the Unicorn Theatre for Children and Brian Way's work at Theatre Centre, again both picked up in Wood's foreword. Bennett's seminal collection of essays identified not only the distinctions between TYA practices across the constituent parts of the UK, but also the wide range of forms that such practice takes. Crucially, Bennett links the development of these practices to the work of Theatre in Education (TiE) companies, specifically at the Belgrade Theatre, Coventry.

This lineage is identified too by two of the contributors to this volume, David Broster and Geoffrey Readman. This lineage has meant that much TYA work shares with TiE an overt concern with the development of the child spectator, cognitively or affectively. Any distinction between the two is frequently blurred in practice, but it may be helpful to identify TYA with the approach identified by Dunlop *et al* as part of the Starcatchers Research Project, where 'the emphasis for the artist is on child development linked to creative and aesthetic awareness and growth, rather than being focused on more formal educational considerations' (2012:12). This also helps to distinguish the underpinning values of TYA from commercially-driven forms of entertainment, including television spin-offs and pantomimes.

The richness and variety of TYA work is captured in Paul Harman's *A Guide to UK Theatre For Young Audiences* (2009), which serves as a companion to Bennett's book, providing a directory of over 150 organisations involved in TYA. These include dedicated venues such as Polka Theatre, the Unicorn Theatre, and the Half Moon in London or the egg in Bath, that make theatre accessible and promote original work of high artistic quality. Other venues, including the National Theatre, have had a long history of producing work for children within their broader repertoire, particularly in adaptations, alongside various programmes run by its education department, as James Reynolds's chapter in this volume outlines. Likewise, Glasgow's Citizens Theatre has a dedicated company, TAG, making work for children and young people. M6 Theatre Company (England), Cahoots NI (Northern Ireland), Catherine Wheels (Scotland), and Theatr Iolo (Wales) are all examples of touring theatre companies working with a deep knowledge of their audiences and a commitment to innovative and exciting forms of production.

For many such companies, festivals are a key part of the TYA landscape, providing opportunities to reach new audiences and for artists to exchange and reflect on their practices. The international character of Imaginate in Edinburgh, Belfast Children's Festival, Darlington's Take Off Festival and The Spark Children's Arts Festival in Leicester, for example, has had a significant impact on the development of the forms and practices of UK TYA practitioners. Likewise, growing awareness of the cultural diversity within the UK itself has enabled and encouraged TYA practitioners to develop innovative forms of practice that engage with their audiences irrespective of distinctions in race, class or ability. At the same time, companies such as Moby Duck, Dragon Breath Theatre and A Thousand Cranes, enrich the field by drawing on various performance traditions and create work that directly relates to the cultural diversity found in the UK.

As editors, our interest in this work has come from different but overlapping backgrounds. Since 2007 Karian Schuitema has been pursuing her doctoral research project on children's theatre in the UK and the representation of cultural diversity, focusing on aspects of interculturalism, multiculturalism and internationalism. She created the Children's Theatre in the UK Research Network, organising a major conference on TYA in July 2010 at the University of Westminster.

With almost twenty years experience in making different forms of performance and conducting workshops for children as an academic, Tom Maguire has honed his interest in TYA in collaboration with Young at Art by participating in, hosting and organising seminars as part of the Belfast Children's Festival since 2009. Together, our aim has been to build on the work of Wood and Grant, Bennett, Harman and others such as Matthew Reason, to provide a space and context for critical discussions of a breadth of topics relating to TYA. Despite the diversity and vibrancy of practices within the field, TYA remains undeservingly underdeveloped as an area of critical and academic study. Accordingly, we foreground the current academic and creative developments in the UK, while also incorporating an awareness of international practice and research.

Public Policy and TYA

Our desire to develop the attention given to this most public of art forms for young audiences has coincided with and responds to an increased focus on young people within the public sphere and specifically in public policy. With the appointment of commissioners for children and young people in England, Northern Ireland, Scotland and Wales over the last decade, the rights of children to speak and to be heard have become enshrined by statute. Included in these rights are children's rights to access the arts. As Gill Brigg identifies in her chapter here, Article 31 of the United Nations Charter on the Rights of the Child states, amongst other things, the right of children 'to participate freely in cultural life and the arts' (OHCHR, 1989:online). As Geoffrey Readman points out in his chapter, there is at the same time an increasing anxiety about the nature of children and childhood, with the riots in English cities in the summer of 2011 provoking editorials and comment columns speaking of 'feral children' (Philips, 2011:online).

Against this background of ambivalence about the place of children in UK society, the value of the arts in the development of young people has been increasingly articulated. In 2012, Darren Henley's *Report on Cultural Education in England* recommended that,

> At its best, a sound Cultural Education should allow children to gain knowledge through the learning of facts; understanding through the development of their critical faculties and skills through the opportunity to practise specific art forms.
>
> Involvement with cultural activities, whether as an active participant (creating a piece of art or craft, reading a book, making a short film) or actively experiencing an event or place (visiting a heritage site, gallery or museum, seeing how a building works, watching a music, dance, or film performance) can be habit forming for the rest of a young person's life. (2012:12)

Henley is clearly mindful of the need to provide an instrumental justification for cultural education in relation to educational attainment and the requirement for an appropriately skilled workforce if the Creative Industries are to drive economic growth. He notes too, however, that 'The skills, which children acquire through good Cultural Education, help to develop their personality, abilities and imagination. They allow them to learn, how to think both creatively and critically and to express themselves fully' (21012:17). Clearly, this is a key value in TYA practice.

A third dynamic of the current UK context is the economic recession, provoking the recurrence of what Bennett has termed 'the stop-go pattern' of government funding (2005:20). Yet TYA companies have been both resilient and inventive in asserting their right to make work and, crucially, to attract funding to support the production of high quality performances and participatory programmes. M6 Theatre Company, for example, worked with the government scheme, SureStart, on a 10-year programme of theatre for young children and families in early years settings throughout Rochdale. While exploiting the opportunities offered by the capacity to effect social benefits, the company's Dot Wood is keen to emphasise the company's commitment, 'to share a passion for theatre as a very special medium for understanding more about the world and ourselves. Underpinning all our work is a desire to make theatre which touches the hearts and minds of our audiences' (2010:online). Attention to this affective domain of children's development is a consistent feature of TYA artists.

Practices and issues in TYA today

So, there is a widespread commitment to a fundamentally child-centred approach to theatre making. As David Wood points out, 'Theatre for children is a separate art form with qualities that make it quite distinct from adult theatre. It is *not* simplified adult theatre; it has its own dynamics and its own rewards' (Wood and Grant, 1997:5). Wood's account of his own approach to writing demonstrates the ways in which his choices as a writer place the child at the centre of the theatrical experience. This focus on the child is apparent too in work which has been devised for young audiences. In many instances, such devising comes out of a process of collaboration with children themselves, as Peter Wynne-Willson's chapter here on what he terms, 'the *Peter Pan* approach' demonstrates. Schuitema's comparative case studies of *The Lion King* and *Once Upon a Tiger* extends this discussion in contrasting the commercial imperatives of the former with the collaborative approach of the latter to making theatre with children in an intercultural context. Likewise, Dominic Hingorani's chapter on work addressing teenagers from ethnic minorities demonstrates ways in which members of the target audience might collaborate in the making process. Such collaboration is readily apparent too in the work of the artists involved in the Starcatchers project across Scotland. The summary report of the project noted that, 'The artists often described how, during the development of their theatre pieces, they were involved in listening to and interacting with the potential audience, and were influenced by them' (Dunlop *et al*, 2012:19).

While there is an evident commitment by practitioners to a child-centred approach, there are significant challenges in understanding who it is that makes up the TYA audience and the particular needs of a diverse constituency. Common issues are raised when it is impossible to rely on spectators sharing an established theatrical competence. Such spectators may, for a variety of reasons, find the experience of theatrical performance novel, alienating or threatening (Wood and Grant, 1997:21). Matthew Reason's chapter here, likewise, notes the difficulty of any generalised concept of the child which ignores divisions of class, gender or race, for example. Hingorani compares three case studies of approaches to making work for teenage audiences which particularly address the diverse ethnicity of the teenage population of East London.

In his chapter, Tom Maguire proposes that it is impossible to talk of an audience as such and that in order to engage with individual spectators at TYA performances, theatre makers might seek out ways of providing a differentiated experience within a single event. Gill Brigg and Tim Webb's essays explore their creative responses to the challenges of reaching what Webb terms 'impossible audiences', particularly those with complex learning difficulties. Both identify the need to have a detailed understanding of the spectator, with Webb tracing the history of Oily Cart's work, and Brigg providing a case study of a single play, *White Peacock*.

These case studies connect with concerns with dramaturgical strategies of engagement explored in essays by Broster and Readman. Both draw on their own extensive experience of making theatre for children to explore the dimensions of participation by spectators in the theatrical world, examining the kinds of effects which derive from immersion in a fictional setting. Reynolds extends this discussion of dramaturgy in his analysis of adaptations by the National Theatre. As well as outlining the institution's history of using adaptation, he develops Bakhtin's idea of the chronotope to demonstrate how the process of adaptation can amplify the fictional setting by focusing on specific concrete details.

One of the perennial issues of TYA is to demonstrate its value, either within or beyond assertions of the instrumentalist value outlined above. Three distinct approaches are outlined in the chapters by Jan Wozniak, Matthew Reason and Jeanne Klein. Wozniak's research into forms of performative writing identifies ways in which teenage spectators might engage with performances of Shakespeare dialogically, provoking critical responses. Reason outlines the ways in which children's agency as spectators can be made manifest in artistic responses which demonstrate how children produce countersignatures to the performance, thereby making the experience for themselves. Klein charts the ways in which she has used interviews to engage with children's responses to TYA performances, thus providing a methodology for researchers in reception studies.

Inevitably in a book such as this, not every topic or issue is addressed. The neglected issues may be geographical: for example, there are no case studies on TYA in Wales or Scotland specifically. Since many of the chapters were originally presented as papers to the conference convened by Karian Schuitema at The University of Westminster in 2010, they reflect the concerns and practices of the contributors to that event so are a snapshot of a specific moment. Nonetheless, they are representative of the nascent state of studies in TYA in the UK. The support that we as editors have received from, for example, Paul Harman as Chair of TYA-UK, also makes us feel confident that this endeavour will be both of interest in itself and a foundation stone on which further work can now build.

References

Bennett, S (2005) *Theatre for Children and Young People: 50 years of professional theatre in the UK*. London: Aurora Metro Press

Harman, P (2009) *A Guide to UK Theatre For Young Audiences*. London: Aurora Metro Press

Dunlop, A *et al* (2011) *Live Arts/Arts Alive: Starcatchers research report, 2011*. Glasgow: University of Strathclyde

Henley, D (2012) *Cultural Education in England*. London: Department for Culture, Media and Sort and Department for Education

Office of the High Commissioner for Human Rights (1989) *United Nations Convention on the Rights of the Child*. http://www2.ohchr.org/english/law/pdf/crc.pdf March 2011

Philips, M (2011) *Daily Mail*. Britain's liberal intelligentsia has smashed virtually every social value, http://www.dailymail.co.uk/debate/article-2024690/UK-riots-2011-Britains-liberal-intelligentsia-smashed-virtually-social-value.html#ixzz1pa1mXCWe Jan 2012

Wood, D (2010) Dot Wood on ... *One Little Word*. http://www.whatsonstage.com/features/theatre/london/E8831252238634/Dot+Wood++on....One+Little+Word.html March 2012

Wood, D and Grant J (1997) *Theatre for children: a guide to writing, adapting, directing and acting*. London: Faber and Faber

2

There is no audience: meeting the dramaturgical challenges of the spectator in children's theatre

Tom Maguire

Introduction

Few fields of theatrical practice are so resolutely focused on and defined by the audiences they seek to engage as TYA. Indeed, a focus on this audience may be the only thing that practitioners who identify with this field have in common. In this chapter I nonetheless question the assumptions and practices that suggest that a collection of individuals gathered together to watch a performance can be regarded as an audience, particularly when those individuals are young. The exploration here draws on wider discussions of the role and nature of theatre audiences (Bennett, 1990; Freshwater, 2009) as a critical framework to discuss a case study of a TYA project, *The Little Box of Wonders*, created at the University of Ulster in a process involving Drama staff and undergraduate students. I suggest that there may be specific approaches to practice which spring from the recognition of the necessity to provide differentiated experiences for the individual spectators of TYA.

The background

The background to this questioning comes from a variety of experiences of making work for young audiences, predominantly within the context of teaching and researching within higher education in the UK. Two specific examples have prompted this reflection. The first was provoked by watching a performance by Patrick Lynch of his co-scripted *What a Wonderful World* for Lyngo

Theatre at Belfast Children's Festival in 2009. The show's pre-publicity emphasised that this was a 'highly interactive show for the early years you can get your hands on the stuff of creation'. The performance in-the-round was for early years (2 to 5 year olds) and required them to engage at key points, making suggestions and interacting with Lynch as narrator and by touching or handling key objects which they would find in the presentational space or which were distributed to them.

At the performance I attended there was a large group of children from two primary schools. Despite Lynch's repeated invitation to the children to participate, the classroom assistants and parent helpers, along with the teachers, insisted on controlling the interaction, frequently instructing the children as to what they should do and how they should do it. At one point, when the children were collecting cottonwool snowballs to throw at Lynch, two of the helpers grabbed the children and pushed them into their places with instructions not to move, while they gathered the balls instead.

The second, and more extended, example is drawn from *The Little Box of Wonders*. The project had three specific phases: the first, a series of workshops with two local primary schools, delivered by students in conjunction with the class teachers and myself as supervisor; the second a devising phase involving the students as performers and in technical roles supported by university staff. The third phase was the performance of the work in May 2010 at the University's Derry campus as part of the Waterside Theatre's Children's Festival and at the Crescent Arts Centre in Belfast as part of the Belfast Children's Festival.

The narrative concerns two young female cousins, Spag and Hettie, who find themselves trapped in a secret room under the stairs of their granny's house. In this secret room they discover two adults, Alf and Betty, whom granny had locked away for trying to steal from her. They eventually realise that they will have to work together to find a key to open the mysterious and magical box of the title if they are to escape. The box promises to provide the answer to all their problems. They search the room, unable to find the key.

At every performance, spectators immediately spotted the numerous keys hanging from the ceiling to which the characters were oblivious. We did not design the piece to be interactive in any respect. However, during performances in both Derry and Belfast, unprompted the children would call out to direct the characters to the keys. Here again, the adults intervened straight away to quieten the children, sometimes with direct instructions, sometimes with less veiled threats of punishment of what would happen when they got back to school or home.

In each instance, the children acted in accordance with Bennett's observation that theatre 'is an interactive process, which relies on the presence of spectators to achieve its effects. A performance is, of course, unlike a printed work, always open to immediate and public acceptance, modification or rejection by those people it addresses' (1990:72). Taken together, the examples suggest that for many children the experience of spectatorship is one in which adults force conventions of spectating onto them, seeking to imprint specific processes of socialisation. As individuals, the children had sought to respond in ways that the structure of the performances had invited, encouraged, or at least allowed.

The adults in the auditorium, however, were quick to suppress this behaviour in favour of how they wished the children to behave; a process in which the individual spectator was forced to become a member of an audience. In part this may be attributable to the context in which the children were watching the performances. In both instances, their attendance was part of a school activity. The collision in expectations of the schools' adults in charge and the adults making the performance may have arisen directly from a lack of shared values with regard to the different behaviours appropriate to school and at a theatre event.

Theatrical competence and the TYA audience

One of the challenges of TYA is building within a performance, or the possibility of assuming, the understanding of the individual children attending that allows them to have a meaningful experience of the event as a whole. Wood cautions:

> Whereas adults know what they are letting themselves in for when entering a theatre, for some children the expectation may be daunting rather than exciting. Not all children find it natural to sit in rows of seats watching actors on a stage. Do not expect them all to understand immediately the theatrical convention of watching a play performed. (Wood and Grant, 1997:21)

DeMarinis terms the understanding of the conventions of theatre as 'theatrical competence' which he defines as 'the sum total of knowledge, rules, and skills that account for the ability to produce performance texts as well as the ability to understand them' (1993:171). In relation to any specific event, this includes the individual's horizon of expectations which Elam helpfully identifies as 'the spectator's cognitive hold on the theatrical frame, his knowledge of texts, textual laws and conventions, together with his general cultural preparation and the influence of critics, friends, and so forth' (1980:94).

Unsurprisingly, both Lynch and other performers who engage directly with their audiences are strongly aware of the requirement to develop and sustain the frames of their performance with their audiences, and frequently implement specific dramaturgical and performative strategies in order to address it. In *What a Wonderful World*, Lynch, in a dual role as narrator and performer, directly addressed the children and set the parameters of the performance explicitly, using both verbal instruction and modelling for the children the behaviour he was asking them to engage in.

These two aspects, theatrical competence and horizon of expectations, are socially constructed, developed and learned through experience with others, in the formation of interpretive communities (Fish, 1980:171, cited in Bennett, 1990:42). Their social dimensions have enabled historians and theorists of theatre, alongside theatre makers, to elide the distinction between the individual spectator and the group that is the audience, so that the plural 'spectators' and singular 'audience' are used interchangeably and the individual spectator is subsumed within each. Wood, for example, charts how when children watch a performance together, it produces an effect where 'the audience will galvanise itself into one organic being. ... As the play progresses, children often react like a crowd of football spectators' (Wood and Grant, 1997:17). Yet both theatrical competence and the horizon of expectations are held idiosyncratically too, with each spectator exercising them in different ways and to different degrees, according to their individual circumstances. Freshwater makes the point succinctly:

> The common tendency to refer to an audience as 'it' and, by extension, to think of this 'it' as a single entity, or a collective, risks obscuring the multiple contingencies of subjective response, context, and environment which condition an individual's interpretation of a particular performance event. A confident description of a singular audience reaction may do no justice at all to the variety of response among different members of that audience. (2009:5)

The heterogeneous TYA audience

TYA makes the singularity of the spectatorial experience all the more pronounced for a variety of reasons. The first concerns the variation in developmental terms within the age groups present in a TYA audience. Much of our understanding of child development rests on conceptual frameworks that divide the growth of the child into specific phases, aligned approximately to their age. So, for example, we have the Piagetian division of cognitive develop-ment in childhood into the following phases (Berk, 2009:222-61): the sensori-motor stage (birth to 2 years); the pre-operational stage (2 to 7 years); the concrete operational stage (7 to 11 years); and the formal operational stage (11 years and older). This schema aligns with the ways in which TYA makers and producers specify the kinds of audiences they seek to attract. Belfast Children's Festival and Imaginate in Edinburgh, for example, in common with many programmers and companies, provide an indicative audience age range in listings for their events. Nonetheless, it is clear that children do not go through these developmental stages at the same rate and or the same chronological moments.

The second, and related, reason for regarding the TYA audience as hetero-geneous is concerned with additional variations between individual children. Here, I draw on the experience of the first phase of workshops in *The Little Box of Wonders* project. The workshops were part of a final-year undergraduate project in which three students, under my supervision, devised and delivered a scheme of work carried out simultaneously over six sessions in two primary schools in Derry. In previous years staff and students from the university had worked on similar drama-in-education projects with these partner primary schools. The schools' involvement allowed the project to draw on funds from the university's ACCESS funding scheme, since both are identified as having a catchment within areas of social and economic deprivation.

In both workshops, the students worked with a single class group of 10 and 11 year-olds. One group had seventeen pupils, the other twenty five. Workshops for the smaller group were held in the classroom or an adjacent open space and the other group worked in the school hall. The students undertook a number of reconnaissance visits to each class. These allowed them to develop a profile of each set of participants in advance through direct observation and discussion with the class teacher and learning support workers.

In line with the overall brief of the project, students also coordinated the activities within the scheme of work to fit with the rest of the curriculum. In accordance with practice across the United Kingdom, the school curriculum in Northern Ireland is organised for different stages aligned with different age ranges, with children in the workshops working at Key Stage 2 which is set for 8 to 11 year olds.

Even in the reconnaissance phase, significant variations between the children in each class were immediately evident. Some had specifically identified learning needs; some had specific physical impairments; while home backgrounds varied across ethno-religious, cultural, economic and social categories. Access to and experience of the arts in general, and live performance in particular, varied also. Once the workshops began, gendered differences became apparent in the kinds of behaviour exhibited, with boys in both classes more willing to engage in acting out and rough play than girls, whose behaviour was, by contrast, more compliant and approval-seeking. The students noted friendship pairings and separation into friendship groups in both classes. Some of the children were still at the stage 'where the goal of peer interaction is to achieve successful, coordinated play' (Parker and Gottman, 1989, cited in Keenan, 2002:210) while the behaviour of others was predicated on their place within their peer group, a later stage. Confidence in and ability to engage with dramatic play and performance also varied.

One of the most difficult tasks for the student facilitators was to work through approximately the same scheme of work with each class, alongside tailoring individual sessions and activities to the individuals in the room and responding to the enormously differing outcomes generated by the children. Students also had to balance three competing sets of demands: the needs of the individuals, the needs of the group as a whole and the demands of the scheme of work. This was particularly focused through the targets of the learning outcomes that they had negotiated with the class teacher and me as their supervisor. They were required as a result to continuously mediate between a predetermined structure and the experience of working with real individuals in the workshop setting.

Facilitators developed strategies to ensure that the children were treated as far as possible as individuals within a group. This practice was particularly fostered by dividing each class into smaller groups to work together, with the teachers and classroom assistants taking part as co-facilitators of the sub-groups. Providing additional support allowed staff to pay much greater attention to each child in turn within the low-focus sub-groups, where they were able to work in parallel and could acknowledge individual differences. Student facilitators could also attend to the unexpected and creative possibilities offered by individual participants. As the facilitators' confidence grew, they likewise demonstrated a willingness to abandon or deviate from their preparation and pre-planned structures if they were not working for any sub-group or individual, or where activities went beyond what they had anticipated in the planning.

Tailoring a TYA Performance

I have detailed this phase of work to underline the distinctions between the responsiveness to the individual possible (and necessary) within a drama-in-education process and the limitations on flexibility, interaction and responsiveness involved in the performance phase of the project. We created the performance through a three-week devising process which involved four performers, a musician, a technical manager and myself. It began with an initial storyboard for which we generated and rehearsed dialogue and action and a number of set-piece routines. The devising was informed by workshops the students had taken with theatre directors Zoe Seaton (Big Telly Theatre Company) and Paul McEneaney (Cahoots NI) and with choreographer Sandie Fisher, a lecturer in Dance and artistic director of Assault Events; and from materials generated from the workshops in the schools.

An idea that the box might appear empty to anyone but the right person came directly from an exercise set up by McEneaney in a workshop with students. One of the school groups generated an idea of a planet where the aliens could only communicate using the word 'dot' and a series of gestures. This was refined to become a set piece in which the characters consider possible other worlds to which the secret inside the box might lead. The performers themselves also created a number of set piece routines, some verbal and some slapstick.

Combining the work of writer, director and dramaturg, my role was to provide the narrative direction and stimuli towards the devising; to edit and script the materials generated; and to direct the performers to bring a completed show together. A number of general dramaturgical considerations informed this process – which can broadly be defined as the requirement to establish coherent given circumstances for the dramatic world and to remain consistent with them. I derived a more specific set of considerations from my understanding of the target audience, children at Key Stage 2 and above. Using the targets set for Key Stage 2, dramaturgical decisions addressed particular aspects of the children's work in school. The curriculum has a specific dimension entitled 'Thinking, Problem-Solving and Decision-Making', within which targets are set for the child's attainment. The performance was therefore shaped in accordance with two broad principles derived from these targets.

The first was the organisation of the narrative around multiple characters. Rather than provide a single central figure, the narrative presented two central character pairings: Spag and Hettie and Alf and Betty. The latter pair operated as a comic double-act, appearing always and only in relation to each other. By contrast, Spag and Hettie were individuated as characters, each with a separate back story and a distinctive relationship to the audience. References to Granny pointed to her as an ever-present but off-stage figure. All of the characters were involved in conflict, through game playing, argument and, at one point, physical fighting. These conflicts were set up as one-against-one, two-against-two, and three-against-one, providing a range of different configurations.

The arrangement invited the spectator to weigh up the different perspectives at work in generating, sustaining and resolving these conflicts, since no character or position displayed greater insight, integrity or moral judgement than the others. This also meant that the resolution of disputes did not simply privilege simple majority decision-making within the bounds of the narrative. This aspect of decision-making and conflict is a key element in the curriculum; by the end of Key Stage 2 children are meant to 'understand more than one point of view (multiple perspectives)' and be able to 'examine options and weigh up pros and cons (decision-making)' (Partnership Management Board, 2007:43). The arrangement connects also to the fundamental requirement for conflict at the heart of drama.

The second related element is the curriculum's emphasis on problem-solving skills where children should 'try alternative problem-solving solutions and approaches' (Partnership Management Board, 2007:43). The idea of a problem at the heart of any play is not unusual. The dramaturgy set up a series of problems and alternative approaches. For example, as they are stuck behind a locked door, firstly, Spag pleads to be let out. The others then try to use Spag as a battering ram, before they all try to find the key. Even when they discover the keys for the room are hanging from the ceiling, the characters have to figure out how to reach them. They work through various physical contortions to raise each other up to detach the keys. The characters try a variety of solutions which expose their limitations, but in doing so they invite the spectators to identify with different approaches to the issues. While the narrative presented collaboration as more effective than self-serving approaches, it is Hettie unilaterally making an unselfish act without influence from the others that brings about the final resolution.

A third element which informed the dramaturgy, but came from outside the curriculum, was derived from my own experience of working and playing with children of this age group (including my own children); from my knowledge of children's literature (Edward Lear, Lewis Carroll, Roald Dahl and Dr Seuss); and from my own study of child development: an emphasis on word play. According to Geller:

For the primary years, then, nonsense play represents a specific method for exploring the nature of the language system. Conceptually ... youngsters are often engaged in the process of confirming how things work by exploring how they don't. In language play, this frequently means describing a world that doesn't exist – telling it like it isn't – as a way of exhibiting mastery over what *is*. (1985: 42)

Throughout, the characters play with different forms of language in ways directly relevant to this age range. The word play begins with the character names, and includes the naming of the only male character as Betty. Two sequences for making decisions are based on joke formats. In one, Alf and Betty compete with 'Knock-Knock' jokes to see who will have to fetch Betty's coat; in another Spag competes against the other three in a 'Doctor-Doctor' joke sequence to see who will have control of the Little Box of Wonders. Alf and Betty's story of how they came to be locked in the room is delivered as if they are in agreement but each contradicts the other throughout:

Betty: It was years ago
Alf: Yesterday
Betty: We were called in to do a big job
Alf: It was only supposed to take 20 minutes
Betty: A cute old Granny with grey hair let us in
Alf: She was a lovely Granny with white hair
Betty: She had lovely circular glasses
Alf: I thought she'd pretty good eye-sight for an old lady
Betty: She had a cute pink cardigan on
Alf: Aww, I remember her cute blue jumper
Betty: She brought us into the kitchen and offered us tea
Alf: So we sat down and drank our coffee.

These examples demonstrate how the production of the play was the result of a carefully thought out and applied set of dramaturgical principles that tailored it closely to the audience for which it was intended. The problem remained that, on their own, such principles still treated the children as a homogeneous group.

This approach would be tested even further since, in addition to the general factors outlined above, the contexts of production in which the play was staged were so distinct. Local primary schools, including the two we had worked with during the workshops, made up the bulk of the audiences at the performances in the university in Derry. However, the specific class groups with which we had worked were to attend the Belfast performances as part of a day trip. The audience was therefore made up of everyone except the very spectators we had worked with. Secondly, the venue for the Belfast performances, the Crescent Arts Centre, is located between the city's central business district and affluent southern suburbs. While schools from other areas and individual family groups attended these performances, there is a significant class distinction between the venue's normal catchment area and the areas from which the Derry schools draw their pupils: a gap in Bourdieuian cultural capital.

Strategies for differential dramaturgies

In attempting to address the needs of individual spectators, we considered two further dimensions in our approach to the dramaturgy: that the spectator would understand the conventions of the performance irrespective of their theatrical competence; and that their modes of accessing the performance would be addressed. One response to the issue of competence was a decision to work with a convention in which characters are able to convey information and situations directly, without breaking out of the frame of the dramatic world by explicitly acknowledging the spectators' presence. Much of the exposition work, for example, is carried in the dialogue, with characters explaining to each other the givens of the fictional world in order to establish some of the conventions of the narrative.

Key information was repeated throughout the performance; constant references are made to Granny's hatred of stealing and her ferocious temper, for example. At the same time, the musician, playing a piano keyboard and situated stage right on the edge of the performance space, was able to develop a direct relationship with both audience and performance, acting as a mediator. In character as Peggy the Pianist, she provided the usual safety announcement at the start of the performance, for example, while her accompanying music, composed alongside the devising process, also cued specific responses to the situations and provided a guiding commentary.

The role of the musician points also to the ways in which the perceptual preferences of individual children might be engaged. Fleming and Mills developed the work of others on learning styles to identify four specific aspects of 'sensory modality' which, they have argued, influence individual learning: visual, aural, reading, and kinaesthetic (1992:138). Theatrical performance provides clear opportunities to address these preferences through its multimodal forms of performance.

It was important within the performance to provide as many opportunities as possible to ensure that each sensory modality was facilitated. In accordance with Fleming and Mills' Read/Write mode which captures a preference for printed words, spectators were given a short programme as they came into the auditorium which included a series of written questions to cue their watching and frame the performance. The sheet also included some jokes and a word search grid.

Another approach was adapted from Brecht's practice of gestus, which was used instead of a wholly psychological approach to gesture, to ensure that the physicalisation of the actors expressed the key relationships in each scene. This connected to the original storyboard technique in the devising process so that each scene had a clear physical expression that communicated its purpose in terms of both narrative and situation. Blocking and movement patterns demonstrated the same action and information as the dialogue, serving to engage both aural and visual modalities. Wood notes too that 'children are intrigued by the body's mobility and virtuosity' (Wood and Grant, 1997:58). The use of music to amplify or express an attitude to the action appealed similarly to the aural mode. Equally, while the children were not taking part physically, our approach to gesture as expressive of a whole situation, rather than being defined by the boundaries of realism was intended to engage the kinaesthetic modality. Fleming and Mills note that this perceptual preference is:

> related to the use of experience and practice (simulated or real). In that sense it is not a single mode because experience and practice may be expressed or 'taken in' using all perceptual modes – sight, touch, taste, smell and hearing. However, a kinesthetic teaching experience is defined as one in which all or any of these perceptual modes are used to connect the student to reality, either through experience, example, practice, or simulation. (1992:139-40)

Theatrical performance fundamentally addresses this perceptual mode. It is worth reflecting that the two examples of participation cited at the outset may well be viewed as the result of a successful appeal to this mode. Spectators who shouted out or tried to engage with the performance were not demonstrating a failure of competence in relation to the role of the audience; they were engaging in a kinaesthetic response to the stimulation provided by each performance.

In suggesting that *The Little Box of Wonders* addressed these different perceptual modes, I propose that this was a specific means of providing a differentiated experience for individual spectators. Certainly, feedback work from our two primary school groups in the form of art work identified very different elements of the performance that appealed to individual children. Problematically, it was not possible within the scope of the project to evaluate the impact these strategies had specifically on each child, and this indicates a gap in the research methodology around this practice.

However, we did monitor the spectators during the run and qualitatively assessed their engagement. The taxonomy developed by the Starcatchers project team around 'engagement signals' is useful to categorise our recorded observations. Spectators were consistently 'attuned' – 'watching, tracking and cued in to what is going on' – 'absorbed' – where the spectator shows 'intense attention for a period [of time] and ignores any distraction' – and 'responsive' – exhibiting 'positive body language, social referencing, following verbal and non-verbal narrative and smiling/reaching/nodding' (Dunlop *et al*, 2011:25).

Crucially, and in relation to the two incidents with which this chapter began, individual spectators were 'instigative' – they sought to provoke 'action in others through own responsive action or vocalisation.' The very behaviour which shows that the individual spectators are engaged in a performance may turn out to be precisely the behaviour which adults want to suppress to turn children into an audience.

Conclusion

I designed the dramaturgy of the final performance of *The Little Box of Wonders* to specifically engage with the challenge of recognising the differentiated nature of the audience. This was not to substitute educational or child development theory for an aesthetic sensibility, but to harness such theory in the development of the production's aesthetic. In tracing out the issues which arise when making a performance that acknowledges that each TYA spectator will have specific needs and competence, I have sought to capture and highlight the kinds of considerations that may already be taken into account implicitly by many practitioners (Wood and Grant, 1997). In making these considerations explicit, I have further demonstrated some ways in which theoretical frameworks can inform performance practice and articulated a value for a dynamic dialogue between research from different fields and the practices of making theatre, not so much for a young audience as for young spectators.

References

Bennett, S (1990) *Theatre Audiences: a theory of production and reception*. London: Routledge

Berk, L E (2009) *Child Development*. Boston: Pearson Education

DeMarinis, M (1993) *The Semiotics of Performance*. Trans. A. O'Healy. Bloomington: Indiana UP

Dunlop, A *et al* (2011) *Live Arts/ Arts Alive: Starcatchers research report, 2011*. Glasgow: University of Strathclyde.

Elam, K (1980) *The Semiotics of Theatre and Drama*. London: Methuen.

Fleming, N D and Mills, C (1992) Not another inventory, rather a catalyst for reflection. *To Improve the Academy* 11, pp.137-155 [online] http://www.vark-learn.com/documents/not_another_inventory.pdf January 2012

Freshwater, H (2009) *Theatre and Audience*. Basingstoke: Palgrave Macmillan

Gellar, L G (1985) *Wordplay and Language Learning for Children*. Urbana: National Council for Teachers of English

Keenan, T (2002) *An Introduction to Child Development*. London, Thousand Oaks and New Delhi: Sage Publications

The Little Box of Wonders (2010) by T Maguire and the company. Directed by Tom Maguire. University of Ulster. Foyle Arts Building, Derry and Crescent Arts Centre, Belfast. May

Partnership Management Board (2007) *Thinking Skills and Personal Capabilities for Key Stages 1 and 2*. Belfast: CCEA

What a Wonderful World (2009) by M Chiarenza and P Lynch. Directed by Marcello Chiarenza. Lyngo Theatre with the Lyric Hammersmith and the Lighthouse Poole, YouthAction Building, Belfast. May

Wood, D and Grant, J (1997) *Theatre for children: a guide to writing, adapting, directing and acting*. London: Faber and Faber

3

The possibility of theatre for children

Matthew Reason

Introduction

The introduction to Jacqueline Rose's *The Case of Peter Pan* contains one of the most notorious assertions about any art for children. 'Children's fiction' writes Rose, 'is impossible, not in the sense that it cannot be written (that would be nonsense), but in that it hangs on an impossibility, one which it rarely ventures to speak. This is the impossible relation between adult and child' (1984:1). Rose's book uses J. M. Barrie's *Peter Pan* as a fulcrum to explore adult fantasies of childhood and her argument is, far more extensive and complex than this introductory statement alone.

However, although Rose barely mentions theatrical productions of *Peter Pan* and is primarily concerned with published literature, her statement is a useful provocation for exploring some of the ideological issues at stake in theatre for children: particularly concerning the power relations between adult and children, and questions of how young audiences are able to construct meaning from the performances they witness. Rose's statement of ideological impossibility is a valuable critique to consider in the context of all culture produced by adults *for* children and young people. To this end in this chapter I first explore a little further what Rose means by the impossibility of children's literature and consider how it might be related to theatre for children. Later I engage with qualitative audience research conducted with young audiences to explore notions of ownership and interpretation in children's lived experiences of theatre. I assert the central necessity of engaging with such reception processes in order to fully understand what theatre for children entails and to seriously confront claims of ideological impossibilities.

Spoken for, not speaking

For Rose, the impossibility of children's literature rests on a number of over-lapping ideological positions. She rightly points out the difficulty of any generalised concept of the child that might exist outside of divisions of class, culture, gender or literacy. Instead, while children's literature is invariably about children – containing stories and adventures involving children – the image of childhood presented is an idealised construct motivated by adult desires: 'if children's fiction builds an image of the children inside the book, it does so in order to secure the child who is outside the book, the one who does not come so easily within its grasp' (Rose, 1984:2).

The image of the child and childhood constructed in children's literature, Rose argues, is of a kind of innocence and asexuality that adults desire as a means of 'prolonging or preserving ... values which are constantly on the verge of collapse' (1984:44). Here Rose is drawing on Philippe Ariès' (1979) influential historical tracing of the invention of a myth of childhood, central motifs of which include innocence, vulnerability and the need for protection and nurturing in the formative, educational years. For Rose, children's litera-ture is not a passive reflection of this cultural conceptualisation of the child but a central means through which images of childhood are regulated (1984: 139). Children's literature, in the end, is impossible because it is less about what children want or need and more about what 'adults, through literature, want or demand of the child' (1984:137).

Rose's claims are provocative and have proved influential, attracting both support and rejection in equal measures (Rudd and Pavlik, 2010). Certainly her arguments are important and the assertion of conceptual impossibility is one that cannot be ignored in the context of theatre for children. If children's literature, as Rose writes, 'sets up a world in which the adult comes first (author, maker, giver) and the child comes after (reader, product, receiver)' (1984:2), with theatre for children the adult also comes first (writer, director, performer) and the child after (subject, audience, receiver). Rose's central focus on adult projections of childhood in children's literature is motivated by the fact that it is adults who purchase books for children. If anything, the economics of theatre for children – the greater resources required, the more public and social context, its status as a treat or special event – make these arguments even more valid with theatre than with literature.

The impossibility of theatre for children invites us to recognise the impossi-bility of thinking of children as a single homogenous group, outside of class, race, religion or gender, and of how a single identity of childhood that might seek to elide these differences could only be constructed from outside of the child herself. The impossibility of theatre for children asks us to explore how childhood itself is an adult construct that is constituted in part through art, literature and theatre. The impossibility of theatre for children requires us to acknowledge the unequal power relationship between adult and child, with children in our society largely constructed as powerless and vulnerable, in need of protection and needing to be spoken for. This speaking for children takes place in theatre for children, in literature for children and in other cultural products produced by adults for children.

Klein echoes these perceptions and writes that 'what might be taken as children's culture has always been primarily a matter of culture produced for and urged upon children. ... Childhood is a condition defined by powerlessness and dependence upon the adult community's directives and guidance' (1998: 95). Klein suggests that the notion of culture for children requires a silenced child whose voice is assumed by adults, a muteness that largely equates to powerlessness over those cultural experiences. The questions this leaves us with are therefore: does this conceptualisation of child audiences as powerless have credence in practice and is this powerlessness absolute when it comes to how children perceive, interpret and play with their cultural experiences?

In her discussion of children's literature Rose makes the following brief passing comment: 'I am not, of course, talking here of the child's own experience of the book [*Peter Pan*] which, despite all attempts which have been made, I consider more or less impossible to gauge' (1984:9). This statement is not elaborated on, but it introduces a second impossibility that is equally telling. Although the exact nature of any individual's experience of art is extremely challenging for anybody else to access, raising many philosophical questions about the nature of the aesthetic experience (Belfiore and Bennett, 2007), one would be highly unlikely to state so confidently that an adult's experience of any particular book was impossible to gauge. Rose is, therefore, perpetuating a disempowering of children – as spoken for, not speaking – while at the same time reiterating the positioning of children as a kind of unknowable other. Rudd also raises these points in 'Children's Literature and the Return to Rose' where he argues that 'children's fiction is only really impossible if we see children as distinct from adults, standing outside society and language, rather than being actively involved in negotiating meaning' (2010:290-1).

The concept of literature or art or theatre *for* children situates children as the receivers and audience, which can be perceived as a largely passive and disempowered position: watchers rather than actors; observers rather than participants. The theatre audience is, literally and typically, required to be silent, only heard at appropriate moments. Yet this depiction of control ignores that the processes of reception are fluid and the position of receiver an active one. As Bennett observes, audiences 'are trained to be passive in their demonstrated behaviour during a theatrical performance, but to be active in their decoding of the sign systems made available' (1997:206). The child audience is just as active in this process of decoding as an adult one is, and, as Rudd (2010) points out, adults cannot simply control the detail or nature of this response. If we consider that children have agency and subjectivity over their own experiences, then culture for children becomes more ideologically possible: not necessarily in its moment of creation, which remains largely for children and by adults, but certainly in its moment of reception.

Researching the audience experience

The surface stillness and passivity of the theatre audience is a public appearance that hides the specific nature of any one individual's lived experience. Exactly what an audience member is thinking or how they are responding to and interpreting a performance is largely concealed and easily labelled too problematic or even impossible know. It inevitably becomes all too commonplace to speak for the audience; to theorise, generalise and assert the nature of the experience – or even to deny that it is relevant at all. This occurs with all theatre, and indeed with much literature and art generally. Hobart writes: 'Audiences rarely get to speak for themselves where it matters. Privileged knowing subjects usually enunciate for them or on their behalf' (2010:204). With child audiences the added dynamic is of course power, with the privileged knowing subject inevitably being an adult who speaks for the experience of the child.

Engagement with audiences is something that theatre studies as a discipline has been largely happy to ignore, whether in the context of adult or children's theatre. As Ginters observes, 'spectators have historically been the least studied and most generalised' of all elements of theatre (2010:7). With theatre for children the requirement to engage with actual audience experiences is made urgent by the potential risk of otherwise fulfilling Rose's description of ideological impossibility. If we do not pay careful attention to the experiences of actual child audiences, not only is theatre for children produced by adults, its meanings, values and reception processes are additionally defined by adults as the knowing subject who enunciates for the absent child.

The challenge of finding out from young audiences the detailed and specific nature of their lived experiences of theatre is one I undertook in depth for my book, *The Young Audience: Exploring and Enhancing Children's Experience of Theatre* (2010). I was interested in what it was possible to uncover about how children watch, remember and process theatre performances. The key ideological and methodological focus of this was to explore the experience of theatre *as theatre*, to focus on the aesthetic, social and empathetic experiences of watching theatre rather than to consider questions of instrumental benefit or educational value.

My research was structured through visual arts workshops in which children were asked to respond through drawing and painting to a performance they had just witnessed. During the workshops, myself and the other workshop facilitators moved around the room talking to individual children as they drew or finished a picture, asking them to tell us about their drawing and through that their experiences of the theatre production. Our conversation with the children was deliberately open, often beginning with a question along the lines of 'tell me about your drawing?' This was followed by questions or conversation as led by the child, the drawing, or the performance being discussed.

As Mayall notes, if the objective is to understand the perceptions and lived experiences of children, it is vital to recognise and work with the knowledge that children already have, at least in experiential terms, of what it means to be a child: 'I want to acquire from them their own unique knowledge. ... I present myself as a person who, since she is an adult, does not have this knowledge' (2000:122).

From the mass of material this approach elicited I sought to trace and analyse particular threads describing the nature of young audience's theatrical experiences. These included a description of how young audiences possess a strong and self-aware (if sometimes latent) theatrical competence; how, while typically lacking the vocabulary through which to easily articulate their knowledge, young audiences are able not only to decode the stage performances but also to analyse and reflect on their decoding (that is, to a degree, to say *how* they know what they know); finally, young audiences engage with both the illusion and material reality of a performance, interested in imaginatively completing a story or illusion in their minds and figuring out how something was done and appreciating of the skill and technique involved.

Much more could be said about these findings and the methodological philosophy behind them. I have explored this in detail elsewhere (Reason, 2010) and do not repeat this reflection here. Instead I focus on those particular moments when the children seemed to claim the performance for themselves, when in acts of rebellion or playfulness or empathy or creativity they made the theatrical experience their own. In focusing on these moments I present them as instances that demonstrate, with regards to Rose, how theatre for children can become ideologically possible through the active agency of the young audience. I draw on Rudd's description of how we need to focus on processes of consumption, on the retelling, editing and customising that children engage in and the ways in which 'children themselves rework stories' to make them their own (2010:298).

The active audience

In my research with young audiences I asked children to remember, draw and talk about a performance they had seen. In some instances they had seen it that morning; in others the day before. In all cases it was no longer there. This is the nature of the theatre performance which, as Peter Brook puts it, 'is an event for that moment in time, for that audience in that place – and it's gone. Gone without a trace' (Brook, 1969-70; cited Melzer, 1995:148). However, while the performance may have gone, a trace does in fact remain in the memories of audience members. Recognition of the memorial afterlife of performance is most succinctly expressed by Eugenio Barba, who writes that 'the performance is the beginning of a longer experience. It is the scorpion's bite which makes one dance. The dance does not stop when you leave the theatre' (1990: 98).

This is as much the case with children as it is with any other audience, with repetition and imitation of things seen in performance one of the most common ways in which theatre continues to resonate with young audiences. In research I have carried out, children have repeated their favourite lines from the performance, hummed along to tunes and mimicked the sound effects or funny voices they had heard:

> Eilidh: And she was very very sad and went down on the ground and screamed.
>
> Sophie: The man said she was very sad and then and then he went waaaahhh!
>
> Eilidh: And then he said, she wasn't that sad, she was just upset. And then she went, ewww ewww... Sophie I'm doing an impression.
>
> Sophie: Of what?
>
> Eilidh and Sophie: Ewww ewww (both mock crying together, with actions)

28

As with this kind of verbalisation or re-enacting, children frequently structure their memories of a performance around favourite instances or moments, which might be considered favourite instances precisely because they can be re-enacted and taken ownership of. It is the potential for repetition, and the act of repetition, which makes them successful as much as anything inherent in the moment itself. They become favourite moments in particular because they can be re-enacted, as in the above example, with friends and therefore mark a shared and stronger group experience and peer identity.

In the exchange above Eilidh and Sophie were re-enacting a scene from *Them With Tails*, a production by English theatre company Tall Stories in which two performers related various fantastical, mythical stories, using both improvisational comedy and storytelling and with varying degrees of input from the audience. One of the stories was of a Clay Pot Boy, who intoned 'I'm still hungry' no matter how much he ate. Several of the children who saw the performance remembered and repeated this line, both individually and in chorused groups, and for some it became the central feature around which they structured their memories and drawings. Lines like these become catchphrases for young audiences, acting much like catchphrases across popular culture which help shape our memories and are vital in establishing a sense of communal experience.

Sometimes these elements of recreation were also physical. On one occasion in a workshop conducted after watching *The Attic under the Sky* by Carte Blanche of Denmark, a number of boys rolled around on the floor while making machine gun noises and gesticulating blood spurting out of their bodies, imitating the exaggerated bodily movements of a death scene in the performance. In thinking about this physicalised response, I have suggested elsewhere (Reason, 2008) that children's embodied re-performances of scenes indicate an ability to read a performance beyond their ability to talk about it. In this instance they knew precisely why the exaggeration of the death scene made it funny, intuitively understanding the appeal of hyperbole, but could not argue this linguistically. Their gameplay also connects with the rough and tumble of boys' play and gave them tacit permission to show off their play-deaths in classroom. It further shows theatre for children – marked by formality, artistic properness and occupying a position between the worlds of adult and child – moving into the child's own realm of play.

For much of the research I have conducted into young audiences, the principle methodological tool has been drawing. This has inevitably shaped the ways the children responded and the ways in which they played with and transformed their experience. Being asked to make a picture of their experience requires participants to do several things: select which moment they want to draw, choose what kind of materials to use, and finally remember and think about what they have seen. As Adams and Baynes discuss, drawing is an activity that can be used to help us look more closely at something and 'develops children's powers of observation, analysis and description' (2003:8). As well as being a process that enhances observation, drawing, they also point out, typically requires us to be inventive and creative in our response. Sometimes this is through happy accident (the unintentional mark or slippage being incorporated into our picture); at other times through a more conscious or playful desire to add and change and construct new scenarios in our drawing (2003:22).

Some additions and innovations might seem banal and yet they contain within them impulses towards creative play and transformation. From my research, examples include a boy who was so disappointed in his picture of a goose (he was drawing a scene from *Martha*, also by Catherine Wheels) he transformed it into a toy aeroplane. Another found he hadn't enough room on his paper for the 100 dogs the story demanded so instead just drew one. The boys then constructed spontaneous stories that altered the performance narrative to take into account the new content their drawing had inspired.

In another instance two boys worked together drawing many many pictures of a character from a production of *Psst!* by Teatre Reflexion of Denmark that their class had named Mr Bean. The naming is in itself an interesting moment of assertion of rights of ownership by the children, as the figure had been unnamed in the production and they had selected his name because he hummed to himself in a manner similar to the TV cartoon version of Mr Bean. At one point in their drawing process a pencil slipped or the charcoal smudged and one of the boys drew a line across the middle of his figure's face. They realised that it looked a little like a mask and from that point on they drew many pictures of a new character they called Super Mr Bean.

> Leo: Look! I've accidentally drawn super Mr Bean
>
> Researcher: You've drawn super Mr Bean?
>
> Leo: By mistake, I didn't want to.

The stories which were subsequently invented about Super Mr Bean were not particularly developed or profound; one involved an encounter with a character named Super Mr Fatso and in some ways deviated entirely from the original production. Nor were their drawings spectacular compared to some produced by other children. In any adult assessment of them as a response to the performance they might have been deemed inappropriate or improper. However, in terms of asserting ownership over the experience they were highly significant.

In community and educational theatre there is a convention of distinguishing between work made *for* a particular audience; produced with a community in a collaborative manner; or made *by* participants through their own agency. This for, with or by distinction can be paralleled with distinctions in children's culture: produced *for* children by adults (theatre for children; television programmes for children etc); made *with* children in a participative or collaborative manner; and the 'play culture' or 'children's own culture' produced *by* children with their peers and including such things as playground games, chants and jokes (Mouritsen, 1998:5-6; cited Johanson and Glow, 2011:61). These distinctions cannot be rigidly maintained, because the games and chants that constitute children's own culture inevitably borrow, intertextually and unapologetically, from existing stories, games and references; similarly, culture produced by adults for children draws upon children's own interests and ideas. This is what is happening in the aforementioned example, where a theatre production (*Psst!*) and television cartoon (*Mr Bean*), both made for children by adults, come together with a wider cultural reference of masked superheroes as the stimulus for a peer-based piece of imaginative play.

A further example comes from Ajay and Alastair, two boys who after watching *Them With Tails* by Tall Stories engaged in a process where drawing – conducted very much alongside each other and in dialogue – allowed them to continue the narrative threads and aesthetic styles presented to them. The story they drew involved a sumo wrestler named Bob who lived in a cave and was fighting an army of flying pigs. Having drawn various elements of this in a storyboard style the two boys then drew Bob who they described as follows:

Researcher: What are all these?

Alasdair: Five-storey muscles

Ajay: He's got bigger ones

Researcher: Oh, huge muscles!

Researcher: He's so muscley! You've both got muscles

Alasdair: And he's got muscles on his eyes

Ajay: There!

Alasdair: That's why they're green.

The two boys started from the point provided for them in the performance – that of an archaic and sometimes surreal form. They took flight with these ideas and made them their own, with five-storey muscles and green muscley eyes. On this occasion part of the stimulation was provided by them working in partnership and the fact that the repetition and development of the narrative became a form of interactive play between them.

Equally crucial, while the first impulse was provided for them by the production, this was not complete in itself, as *Them With Tails* did not present on stage a fully realised representation of a sumo wrestler. As Philip Pullman writes, in the moment of watching the audience 'contribute their imagination' (2004) to complete the suggestions made by the performance. This in-the-moment investment of imagination is, of course, ephemeral and we cannot be certain what exactly the children saw in their mind's eye as they watched. The task of drawing after the performance continues this process and, moreover, makes the act of imagination and investment concrete. Asking the children to draw required them all to add to what they had seen and make choices in representation. As they constructed their representations on paper they came to realise that they had a kind of playful power and ownership over the production as it became what they drew and what they imagined.

Countersignatures

The kind of playful responses to theatre performances I have discussed here involve both acts as factual recall and imaginative construction. Children do not limit themselves to things that necessarily happened in the performance, but take those as a starting point for various kinds of innovations and explorations. Here I draw on Derrida's proposal that readers' and spectators' responses to art form a countersignature to the original work, a proposal Caputo elegantly summarises:

> Texts, if there is anything to them, elicit, call for, and provoke other texts – responses, commentaries, interpretation, controversies, imitation, forgeries, plagiarisms, echoes, effluences, influences, confluences, translations, transformations, bald misinterpretations, creative misunderstandings etc. (1997:189)

Audience responses to theatre can be considered a kind of countersignature, containing many of the mutations and transformations Caputo evokes. Such transformations of the work in the audiences' imagination become a new experience and a new work in their own right. In the context of theatre for children this means the work exists not simply in the stage performance, written text or adult production made *for* children, it also exists in the mind and response made by the young audience.

The thing, the work, the performance, is therefore incomplete until it is received, processed and, in a sense, countersigned by the audience. Naturally, these responses are not produced from nothing and here I'd agree with Morley who criticises the way some audience research has 'romanticized the supposed power and freedoms' of spectators (2006:102). Instead, responses are produced by a subtle interplay between individual spectators, their peers, the performances themselves and a whole set of wider cultural experiences and influences. In this manner the richest and most successful theatre experiences shift from being culture *for* children to being children's own culture that is integrated into their creative play and into their sense of identity and self.

It is here that theatre for children becomes possible, not in the sense of simply existing (which is prosaic) but in the sense of mattering and being meaningful. As Johanson and Glow argue, an important element in enhancing children's experiential engagement with the arts 'lies in the valuing of children's critical choices' and a greater understanding of children's own aesthetics (2011:70). The danger of not paying attention to the lived experiences of children is that they become other, outside of language and considerations of personal agency and aesthetics. By engaging in the admittedly complex and methodologically challenging task of exploring how young audiences engage with theatre we can recognise the complexity and richness of their lived experiences.

References

Adams, E and Baynes, K (2003) *Drawing Power Notebooks*. London: Drawing Power, The Campaign for Drawing

Ariès, P (1979) *Centuries of Childhood*. Hammondsworth: Penguin

Barba, E (1990) Four Spectators. *The Drama Review* 34(1) p96-100

Belfiore, E and Bennett, O (2007) Determinants of Impact: Towards a Better Understanding of Encounters with the Arts. *Cultural Trends* 16(3) p225-75

Bennett, S (1997) *Theatre Audiences: a theory of production and reception*. London: Routledge

Caputo, JD (ed) (1997) *Deconstruction in a Nutshell: a conversation with Jacques Derrida*. New York: Fordham University Press

Ginters, L (2010) On Audiencing: The Work of the Spectator in Live Performance. *About Performance* 10 p7-14

Hobart, M (2010) Rich kids can't cry: reflection on the viewing subject in Bali. *About Performance* 10 p199-222

Johanson, K and Glow, H (2011) Being and Becoming: Children as Audiences. *New Theatre Quarterly* 27(1) p60-70

Klein, S (1998) The Making of Children's Culture. In H Jenkins (ed) *The Children's Culture Reader*. New York: New York University

Mayall, B (2000) 'Conversations with Children: Working with generational issues'. In P Christensen and A James (eds) *Research with Children: Perspectives and practices.* London, Falmer

Melzer, A (1995) 'Best Betrayal': The Documentation of Performance on Film and Video, Part 1. *New Theatre Quarterly* 11(42) p147-57

Morley, D (2006) Unanswered Questions in Audience Research. *The Communication Review* 9(2) p101-21

Pullman, P (2004) Theatre – the true key stage. *The Guardian.* 30 March

Reason, M (2008) Thinking Theatre: Enchanting Children's Theatrical Experiences Through Philosophical Enquiry. *Childhood and Philosophy.* 4(7) http://www.filoeduc.org/childphilo/n7/Matthew_Reason.pdf December 2011

Reason, M (2010) *The Young Audience: Exploring and Enhancing Children's Experiences of Theatre.* Stoke on Trent. Trentham

Rose, J (1984) *The Case of Peter Pan: or, the impossibility of children's fiction.* Basingstoke: Macmillan

Rudd, D (2010) Children's Literature and the Return to Rose. *Children's Literature Association Quarterly* 35(3) p290-310

Rudd, D and Pavlik, A (2010) The (Im)Possibility of Children's Fiction: Rose twenty-five years on. *Children's Literature Association Quarterly* 35(3) p223-9

4

Theatre for young audiences at London's National Theatre

James Reynolds

Introduction

Addressing the needs of a nationwide audience is a challenging task for a building-based organisation such as the National Theatre. Yet from its inception, the National was seen as a way of enhancing the delivery of theatre for young audiences. This chapter historicises TYA at the National to identify and analyse the development of significant aspects of practice. It assesses how the remit to be national is met through a range of practices, specifically the development of touring work, externally funded projects and adaptations.

TYA at the National Theatre: roots and trajectories

The Arts Council reported in 1970 that TYA had a 'shabby image', and had 'long been lacking' in London (p28). The proposed National Theatre would 'remedy that deficiency', and hope was even expressed for a second young people's theatre in London where experiments with 'informal methods' and 'audience participation' could be undertaken (Arts Council, 1970:28). Two new centres would put heart 'and new hope into all the people who have laboured so long in a rather stony vineyard' (Arts Council, 1970:28). The Theatre Centre, which the report identified as deserving of this second venue, celebrated its 50th anniversary in 2003. The idea that the National would provide a home for TYA came to be realised in a very different way.

Prior to the opening of the South Bank venues in 1976, the National Theatre Company worked at the Old Vic. Under Frank Dunlop, an associate director of the National, they had built up a strong practice of TYA as the Young Vic Company, first formed in 1947 'to offer work to promising young actors and to play for young people' before disbanding in 1951 (Roberts, 1976:136). Dunlop successfully revived the company in 1970, and when the South Bank theatres opened it became the 'natural heir' to take over the Old Vic as a TYA venue (Roberts, 1976:190).

The Young Vic Company's inaugural production, Scapino, Dunlop's adaptation of Moliere's *Les Fourberies de Scapin*, undertook 'an award-winning tour of Europe' (Goodwin, 1988:13-4). Their temporary residence was 'a converted butcher's shop' on The Cut and in May 1976 it was announced that it would 'take over the Old Vic tenancy with an Arts Council subsidy' in 1977 (Roberts, 1976:190).

The move to the Old Vic never materialised however and momentum was lost at a key moment, despite recognition of the need for TYA and recommendations for funding it. The loss of this initiative meant that TYA at the National would have to compete with main house productions for resources. While this may seem disadvantageous, it ensured that TYA was regularly programmed on the National's stages, almost from the outset.

In the early days of the National, director Michael Bogdanov championed TYA and his Christmas show, *Sir Gawain and the Green Knight* (1977), was its first in-house production for children (Goodwin, 1988:20). Bogdanov built on this success by adapting *Hiawatha* (1980) which was popular enough to revive 'several times'. The adaptation became 'the National Theatre's first national tour for children' (Goodwin, 1988:22). Bogdanov followed it with *The Rhyme of the Ancient Mariner* (1984).

Adaptations for children have a long history at the National but whereas Bogdanov and Dunlop's adaptations were of classic or character-based texts, recent adaptations have been of contemporary texts with significant contemporary resonance. Furthermore, the success of the touring work set a precedent for subsequent TYA tours. A new education department was opened which began to establish significant engagement with a young national audience. All this made the 1980s a key period in which the three trends that I address in turn – touring, externally funded projects and adaptations of children's literature – were consolidated.

The touring practice developed in two major ways. In 1982 the education department arrived at a successful model with a production of *The Caucasian Chalk Circle*, which toured to approximately twenty towns and cities. Such theatre classics could be cast with a 'variety of accents' to meet the needs of diverse regional audiences, and presented in 'modern and accessible' versions (Clarke, 2008:176-7). Between 1982 and 1988 the education department 'staged ten more productions which ranged from Shakespeare to contemporary writers and one-man shows' (Goodwin, 1988:23).

These Mobile productions were the first major development in terms of the National's practice of touring its TYA work. Mobile shows toured to secondary schools, usually on a run of nine to fifteen weeks and concluded with a three week run in the Cottesloe. Although a key strategy in engaging a younger audience across the nation, Mobile productions ceased in 2005 with a production of Brian Friel's *Translations* (2005). The cancellation was a loss to young audiences around the country.

The National's model of funding is worth noting here. From 1992-3 despite receiving £10.89 million for its core costs – the largest Arts Council grant that year – only £200,000 financial support was allocated for touring programmes (Shank, 1994:185). Mobile productions depended upon external funding streams that were not renewed and the National still seeks a similar funding arrangement in its attempts to revive them. Touring seems an obvious means for the theatre to qualify as national, but TYA tours are often dependent upon external funding. Regional tours of main house productions or even live transmissions of such performances to regional cinemas are less vulnerable, but do not always meet the needs of young audiences. Main house TYA is toured far less frequently than adult theatre and is more likely to be transferred to another London theatre than to tour nationally. The National's cinema broadcasts began only recently with a screening of *Phèdre* (2009). Although main house TYA works such as *Nation* have been broadcast (2010), the medium does not offer the crucial exposure to live theatre that young audiences need.

Renamed Discover in 2008 and, more recently, as National Theatre Learning, since 1996 the education department has also produced a second form of touring TYA, Primary Classics, which became Primary Theatre in 2010. Primary Theatre tours around 40 primary schools and uses performance to help young children in develop 'key literacy and social skills alongside a knowledge of how theatre is created' (RNT, 2011). It also delivers a shortened Shakespeare play for children over 7. Titles have ranged from *Macbeth* (2009) to *Twelfth Night* (2010), although the project's renaming reflects the intention to produce a wider range of work in the future.

The perception that institutions like the National represent cultural privilege and class division requires such institutions to engage self-reflexively with their social meaning, with what Nicholson calls 'the politics of place' (2009: 59). The National's touring work undoubtedly helps erase the status of its own place-hood as a 'nostalgic marker of social stability' (Nicholson, 2009:63). Nevertheless, it is difficult to see how, without Mobile productions, the National can share in the democratic ambition of TYA to counter what Nicholson describes as 'some of the more prejudicial meanings associated with ... theatre as a cultural institution' (2009:59), despite its success in opening the doors of its own theatres to young people. It may be that the availability of learning programmes for young audiences that now accompany nationwide tours, alongside the digital content available about the National's work online, will ameliorate potential issues of access and entitlement.

As the cancellation of Mobile productions shows, the creation of TYA at the National is partly dependent on securing external funding, although other forms of TYA supported by these sources have fared better. In 1989 the education department launched the Lloyds Bank Theatre Challenge, a festival scheme that aimed to encourage young people's theatre companies from all over Britain and which culminated in local performances, performances in regional theatres and three showcase nights at the National. From 1994, this was replaced by the still-running Connections scheme. Originally 'a partnership between BT, the National, regional theatres, numerous playwrights and hundreds of young theatre companies', Connections likewise culminated with performances at the National.

In its different forms the education department has maintained and developed a national, new writing, youth theatre festival into its third decade which has become a highly significant TYA practice. Connections plays speak directly to the lives and issues young audiences face, and do so in the context of a national festival. Perhaps more than in any other of its TYA, Connections sees the National as national, and, crucially, as placing a new, vigorous tradition of theatre into young people's cultural lives.

Connections has added a further ten plays to the TYA repertoire year on year, and constitutes 'a key component' of the National's outreach work (Deeney, 2007:331). Schools, colleges and youth theatres pay to participate in the Connections scheme, but this does not diminish the significance of a nationwide festival of theatre made and performed by young people for young audiences. These plays 'provide creative and intellectual challenges' for young actors and young audiences alike, and the principle of the scheme could only be significantly enhanced by restoring its now defunct global element, International Connections (Nicholson, 2009:53).

New territories since 2003

At the same time as the National's touring programmes and festival work for young audiences have developed, the third trend I examine, the adaptation of novels, has undergone a process of evolution. The National has produced a greater volume of adaptations under Nicholas Hytner than under any of its previous artistic directors. In the fifteen years of Peter Hall's artistic director-ship (1973-1987) twelve adaptations of literary works were staged; when Richard Eyre took over from 1987 to 1997, nine adaptations were produced; a further eight followed in the seven years of Trevor Nunn's leadership (1997-2003); while the first seven years of Hytner's artistic direction (2003-2010) saw the National stage thirteen adaptations (Clarke, 2011).

Almost doubling of the number of adaptations staged reflects an increased engagement with wider culture and has raised the National's profile by con-necting its work to the interests of other kinds of audience. Furthermore, the increased volume gives strong backing to what is often seen as a controversial practice. In both regards, potential benefits are attached, attracting audiences and the attention of the media and public.

The National has traditionally attracted young audiences by staging adapta-tions of children's literature. However, recent adaptations are distinctive not only in terms of volume but also for their nature. Under Hytner, the National has deliberately based its TYA output on adaptations of contemporary chil-dren's fiction which has allowed it to reach out to young audiences in exciting ways. Hytner did not wish to base the National's TYA on Victorian and Edwar-dian classics, as it had in productions like *Wind in the Willows* (1990), *Alice's Adventures Underground* (1994) and *Peter Pan* (1997). On taking up the role, he wanted to create a play for a young audience that would speak 'as directly to a young audience as a movie at the local multiplex' (Butler, 2003:6). He was applauded for his ambition in staking out new territory, rather than 'dusting off an old musical' for Christmas which had been the strategy of his pre-decessor, Nunn (Wolf, 2004:58).

Hytner says that 'teenagers ask the big questions that we have no time to ask for most of the rest of our lives'. He chose to adapt Philip Pullman's *His Dark Materials* in 2003 because it is 'exciting and specifically teenage in the ferment of big, metaphysical ideas' that it offers (Kellaway, 2003:5). Nicolas Wright's adaptation of Pullman's novels therefore attempted to capture the works' seriousness regarding the 'big questions: God, loyalty, the environment, death'; furthermore, Wright describes the belief 'that modern children think about [such questions] just as deeply' (cited in Hunter, 2004 online) as a 'basic article of faith about the show' (Pullman, 2003:13). Whelehan argues that adaptations insert 'literary texts into the same critical sphere as the consumption of more explicitly commercial products', like films, and this enables audiences 'to be more self-conscious about their role as critics' (1999:19). Such plays make a double invitation to be critical, both of the ideas explored within them and with regards to the issue of how best to adapt a literary work for the stage. Such an engagement can be one of considerable complexity, and reward, but the approach is not without risk.

Since 2003 the National has presented a sequence of high-profile adaptations of children's literature in its 'financially crucial Christmas slot' (Wolf, 2004:58). Nearly all the National's main house TYA has been scheduled at Christmas but Hytner's programming, often controversially, has not reflected the spirit of the Christmas season, as had been the case under previous artistic directors. He began with Wright's adaptation of *His Dark Materials* (2003-2005) and continued with Helen Edmundson's adaptation of Jamila Gavin's *Coram Boy* (2005-2007) and Mark Ravenhill's adaptation of Terry Pratchett's *Nation* (2009). Nick Stafford's adaptation of Michael Morpurgo's *War Horse* opened in 2007 and is still in production at time of writing. These shows delivered Hytner's reimagining of the National's approach to a serious-minded young audience. *His Dark Materials* was quickly recognised as 'a landmark in children's theatre' (Halliburton, 2004:63), seen 'by nearly 139,000 people' in its first run alone (Jury, 2004:7). This was 'children's theatre of an uncommon maturity and ambition' (Sutcliffe, 2004:5).

His Dark Materials quickly became an object for media discussion regarding what Morpurgo had christened 'the 'Golden Age' of adult-children crossover literature' (Clapp, 2004:10). Subsequent to the 'Rowling revolution' of the late 1990s, in which children's book sales rose by twenty two per cent worldwide following the success of the Harry Potter franchise, the 'line between children's and adult fiction' had blurred (Rees, 2003:1). Hytner had chosen his source text and strategy precisely and well. There is, he said, a 'new generation of children's writers who treat their readers seriously', and 'we want to do the same' (Kennedy, 2003:10).

By adapting crossover literature, Hytner connected the National to Morpurgo's Golden Age, speaking to, and capitalising on, an emerging audience. 'Epic is back', wrote Sam Leith of *His Dark Materials*, and this year, panto 'may

40

not cut it' (2003:23). The ramifications of this spread beyond the South Bank. Alongside *War Horse* at the National, for example, 2007 saw three further adaptations of Morpurgo's work: *Kensuke's Kingdom* at Birmingham Stage, *Billy The Kid* at the Unicorn and *The Mozart Question* at Bristol Old Vic (Croall, 2008:79).

Such work can achieve considerable complexity but there are risks. Reviewers like Michael Billington 'disapprove of adaptations, and would prefer the theatre to produce new plays rather than rework old books' (Pullman, 2004: 12). Wright's adaptation of *His Dark Materials* was faithful to the event sequence of the novels, and for Charles Spencer, played 'like one damned thing after another', failing 'to develop an independent dramatic life of its own' (2004:17). The intertextuality of Pullman's novels led Billington to question 'the adaptability of Pullman's trilogy' (2004:22). Hytner defended his policy and production, however, saying that he had 'very little patience with the idea that adaptation is an inferior form of art' (Sierz, 2003:3).

Away from the controversies around adaptation, the source texts chosen under Hytner's artistic direction set particular challenges for theatre makers. The worlds of these crossover books are alien, imagined or distant, historically and geographically. In the novelistic form, such content can be unpacked slowly and in detail. Rather than attempting to recreate the worlds of these texts in faithful, naturalistic detail on stage however, the TYA productions use theatrical forms to distil and magnify the most significant features of their source texts. Such forms are often highly stylised rather than mimetic. As Whelehan argues, the movement away from 'fidelity and historical verisimilitude' is significant because it facilitates a deeper conceptual examination of the ideologies of the past (1999:12).

His Dark Materials, Coram Boy, War Horse and *Nation*, which respectively explore serious, ethical themes of religion, slavery, war and colonialism are examples of theatrical adaptations that effectively encourage 'criticism of the processes of ideology' (Whelehan, 1999:12). Rather than attempting mimetic representation, their stylised theatricality amplifies the time and place of their fictional worlds. Through the travels of the horse, Joey, across the battlefields of World War I, firstly in the English cavalry and then the German army, *War Horse* makes the futility and inhumanity of war visible through the form of puppetry. While the production is affecting, its foregrounded theatricality also creates space for reflection.

Each of these fictional worlds has, to use Mikhail Bakhtin's term, a highly distinctive 'chronotope' which makes this device particularly effective. The term describes a fusion of time and space into a 'concrete whole'; in this whole, time 'thickens, takes on flesh, becomes artistically visible', and space 'becomes charged and responsive to the movements of time, plot and history' (Bakhtin, 2000:53). The chronotope grounds character and narrative in 'an actual reality' (Bakhtin, 2000:54), something that is also essential in *His Dark Materials*, where Lyra encounters a continuous stream of fantasy beings in her travels, and escape from the Church.

Bakhtin notes that the chronotope of the road has a particular facility 'for random encounters' between 'representatives of all social classes, estates, religions, nationalities, ages' (2000:54). As a Victorian lady, Daphne in *Nation* would have had little chance of meeting the native Mau without the road. The social permeability of the eighteenth century presented in *Coram Boy* also depends on it and the battlefields of World War I exemplify its capacity to break lives apart and then throw them together again.

It is not only theatrical form which invites an investigation of the ideologies of different times and places, however. These works share a particular affective narrative content which further contributes to their effectiveness. This can be traced to a theme which each of the source novels shares: the rescued orphan. Lyra and Will are both apparently fatherless in *His Dark Materials*; many of the characters in *Coram Boy* have lost parents, most notably Alexander, who orphans himself, and, unknowingly, his unborn child, Aaron, when he runs away from home. In *War Horse* Joey is an orphan once he is sold to the army and separated from Albert, who has cared for him since he was a foal; while in *Nation*, the young Mau loses his parents to a tsunami, and the equally young shipwrecked Daphne must learn to live without hers as well.

The source texts of these plays are odysseys of sorts; rites of passage which see orphaned characters return home or reunited with their families. This narrative content plays upon the emotive subject of the loss of a child or, conversely, a parent. The wealth of textual detail which creates the chronotope in a novel can be produced in theatre by forms which can articulate the ideological atmosphere of a distant time and place.

But these adaptations also appeal because their narratives are both horizontal, tracing the physical sequence of the orphan's journey home along the road, and vertical, slowly articulating the structure of a family. Developing and expanding their significance synchronically and diachronically, they offer different entry points of interpretation for spectators of different ages. The ultimate accolade for *His Dark Materials* was that both adults and children wanted to see it (Kohler, 2009:129). Just as what has been termed crossover literature expanded its readership by offering levels of meaning that were stimulating for adults, the National's adaptations of that literature also crossed over, offering adults and children the satisfactions of serious questions, emotionally powerful narratives and an inventive use of form capable of creating other worlds.

The cultural dynamism of TYA

The works identified are additionally significant because they demonstrate the cultural dynamism of TYA within the National. The productions produced a demand for inventiveness in the use of theatrical forms which in turn demanded fresh ways of telling stories from writers and adaptors. *His Dark Materials* brought expertise and collaboration in puppetry into the National at an unprecedented level; unsurprisingly, the art form featured in each of the next three crossover adaptations.

Crossover books can compel inventive uses of form, particularly if their fictional world is alien, distant or even unimaginable. In *His Dark Materials*, the human characters from Lyra's reality are accompanied by daemons, emanations of individual essence which takes the form of an animal: Lyra's daemon, for example, is a pine marten. The daemons are intrinsic to both character and narrative, and puppetry was a logical choice of form through which to manifest them. Puppets have appeared at the National before, of course. During a Platform discussion in 2004, Hytner noted that the puppeteers ran simultaneous rehearsals to develop the qualities of these puppet characters. For Georgie Brown the 'real triumph' of *His Dark Materials* was the puppetry, which moved 'beyond literary illustration into a wholly theatrical realm' (2004:72).

Equally significantly, these works have contributed to a change in perception regarding puppetry. In *Coram Boy*, it provided the solution through which the birth, live burial and exhumation of a number of babies was given form. Edmundson notes that such 'theatrical convention [was] incredibly liberating' in adapting *Coram Boy* because naturalism alone could not 'cope with the demands of the story' (Croall, 2008:71). In *Nation*, puppets, in the form of animated costumes of vultures and spiders, populate the play's island location. Two of the main characters in *War Horse* are horses, a feature which demanded major collaboration with specialist puppet theatre company, Handspring.

Reflecting on Handspring's work, Mervyn Millar writes that 'only ten years ago puppetry was still largely seen as a medium for children' (2007:47). Handspring's Adrian Kohler says that, at 'European theatre festivals, we would hear English puppet companies complain that audiences were put off by the 'P' word' (2009:130). Through its TYA, however, the National has helped update perceptions of puppetry, and contributed to a renaissance in the form.

The commercial success of *War Horse* further reveals the cultural dynamism of TYA. Lessons were learned following the precedent set by *His Dark Materials*. Despite a continued demand for tickets, even after a revival there was no theatre in the West End that could handle its transfer and a major financial opportunity was lost (Reynolds, 2004:5). *War Horse*, on the other hand, has been transferred and extended by an award-winning remounting in New York. The National's state subsidy for core costs was reduced from £19,220,748 in 2009/10 to £17,462,920 for 2012/13 – a cut of around fifteen per cent in real terms (Arts Council, 2011). But *War Horse*'s commercial success will see that the theatre copes with this. Given the artistic and financial success of these productions, it is reasonable to conclude that TYA at the National has a more than healthy future.

Nicholson identifies 'a synthesis of theatre and education' (2009:12) in contemporary TYA practice, and we can read these productions as balancing art and instrumentality and therefore as an example of this synthesis of aims. I have argued that these works place a key focus on the ideas of their source texts, ideas which are sufficiently engaging to cross over the borders of child-adult interest, and that they use a style of adaptation which engages with serious issues. The balance is accomplished through innovative formal expression, in combination with the treatment of ethical issues such as slavery and war which are made more profound for spectators in being interwoven into affective narrative material.

War Horse reaches its emotional peak with the reunion of Joey and Albert as the war ends for them both. But its expression of the futility of war is underpinned by the insight into the time and place provided by the sophisticated horse puppets. Joey functions as a lens through which the unimaginable horror of millions of human deaths can be conceived of and felt, and thus brought into focus. Furthermore, without a nationality, Joey also functions to show the horror for both warring sides. The pacifist perspective of the work is all the more effective for appearing less as a blunt, predictable message, and more as an empathetic insight into all sides of that horrific experience. Such a work reflects David Hornbrook's belief that it is only when art engages 'with the content and form of dominant ideologies' that the 'necessary aesthetic foundation for a theory of dramatic art' can be achieved (1989:108). The

National's recent main house TYA may therefore provide an aesthetic foundation for theoretical frames regarding the adaptation of children's literature for young audiences.

Conclusion

In some senses TYA at the National has not changed much since the days of Michael Bogdanov and the education department. The theatre still relies upon the adaptation of children's literature as source texts for its TYA, and although Mobile productions await revival, many other programmes are delivered outside of its London spaces. What has changed is the selection and manipulation of source texts to produce TYA which has a contemporary resonance and is ethically engaged, artistically innovative and culturally dynamic. The commitment to using new technologies of live transmission and the internet to create a presence outside of the capital is fresh and supports the tours and transfers of major productions. Nor must we forget the significant level of facilitation for TYA that is made possible through the Connections festival, which brings young performers and young audiences together in a growing and vital culture of theatre.

Finally, we can see how the National has evolved and will continue to evolve towards a synthesis of artistic and instrumental aims. In 2011, Discover was again renamed as National Theatre Learning, an umbrella name which encompasses the breadth of programmes now delivered by the theatre and reflects a commitment to creating greater access. Work is being undertaken to convert prop and workshop spaces into The Clore Learning Centre which will connect directly into the Cottesloe Theatre and open in 2014. The learning programmes of the National, which have always been physically separated from the theatre itself, will be rejoined to it once the theatre celebrates its 50th anniversary in October 2013. The opportunity to become a beacon for TYA that the National Theatre lost when the Young Vic Company were not given the Old Vic has therefore reoccurred. The synthesis of art and instrumentality reflected in the National's TYA and represented across its main house productions and learning programmes will be mirrored within the institution itself, and the National will have achieved its strongest position to date from which to be national for young audiences.

References

Arts Council of Great Britain (1970) *The Theatre Today in England and Wales: the report of the Arts Council Theatre Enquiry.* London: The Arts Council of Great Britain

Arts Council England (2011) *The Royal National Theatre.* http://www.artscouncil.org.uk/rfo/royal-national-theatre July 2011

Bakhtin, M (2000) Mikhail Bakhtin, from The Dialogic Imagination. In M McQuillan (ed) *The Narrative Reader*. Abingdon and New York: Routledge

Billington, M (2004) *Guardian. His Dark Materials*, 22

Brown, G (2004) *Mail on Sunday.* Making Light Work of Such Dark Matters, 72

Butler, R (2003) *The Art of Darkness: staging the Philip Pullman trilogy.* London: Oberon

Clapp, S (2004) *Observer.* Daemons are forever, 10

Clarke, G (2008) *Stage Versions of Literary Works at the RNT.* London: RNT Archive

Croall, J (ed) (2008) *Buzz Buzz: playwrights, actors and directors at the National Theatre.* London: Methuen

Deeney, J F (2007) National causes/moral clauses?: the National Theatre, young people and Citizenship. *RiDE: Research in Drama Education* 12(3) p331-344

Goodwin, T (1988) *Britain's Royal National Theatre.* London: Nick Hern Books

Halliburton, R (2004) *New Statesman.* Just imagine, 63-64

Hornbrook, D (1989) *Education and Dramatic Art.* Oxford: Blackwell

Hunter, P (2004) *Guardian.* More Lyra please. How three writers adapted Pullman. http://www.guardian.co.uk/stage/2004/nov/24/theatre.stage June 2012

Jury, L (2004) *Independent.* Pullman's six hour children's epic returns by popular demand, 7

Kellaway, K (2003) *Observer.* Pullman class, 5

Kennedy, M (2003) *Guardian.* Forget the jolly and the holly – this is Christmas, 10

Kohler, A (2009) *War Horse.* In J Taylor (ed) *Handspring Puppet Company.* Johannesburg: David Krut Publishing

Leith, S (2003) *Daily Telegraph.* The titanic struggles of Tolkien and Pullman put panto in the shade, 23

Millar, M (2007) *The Horse's Mouth: staging Morpurgo's War Horse*, London: Oberon

Nicholson, H (2009) *Theatre and Education.* Basingstoke: Palgrave Macmillan

Pullman, P (2003) *His Dark Materials.* Adapted by N Wright, London: Nick Hern Books

Pullman, P (2004) *Guardian.* Let's pretend, 12-13

Rees, J (2003) *Daily Telegraph.* Books, 1-2

Reynolds, N (2004) *Daily Telegraph.* Dark fantasy overcomes its technical daemons to light up the stage, 5

Roberts, P (1976) *The Old Vic Story.* London: W H Allen

Royal National Theatre (2011) Primary theatre for key stage two. http://www.nationaltheatre.org.uk/61353/primary-theatre/for-key-stage-2.html July 2011

Sierz, A (2003) *Independent.* Enter the daemons, 1-4

Shank, T (1994) The playwriting profession: setting out and the journey. In T Shank (ed) *Contemporary British Theatre.* Basingstoke: Palgrave Macmillan

Spencer, C (2004) *Daily Telegraph.* Working with the wrong materials, 17

Sutcliffe, T (2004) *Independent.* An epic battle of theatre versus cinema, 5

Whelehan, I (1999) Adaptations: the contemporary dilemmas. In D Cartmel and I Whelehan (eds) *Adaptations from Text to Screen, Screen to Text.* Abingdon and New York: Routledge

Wolf, M (2004) *Variety.* Spotlight on dark, 58

5

The Peter Pan approach: creating plays for children from children's play

Peter Wynne-Willson

My grandmother, Theodora Llewelyn Davies, had five cousins who lived in London at the end of the 1800s. They used to visit Kensington Gardens with their nanny, and there they met an interesting little man, Mr Barrie, with whom they would chat and play. Together they made up stories and acted them out. They invented places, ideas and characters, among whom was a boy called Peter Pan. The story of how Peter Pan was created was familiar to me as a child, and is now widely known, having been the subject of a book (Birkin, 1979), a major BBC television series (*The Lost Boys*, 1978) and a Hollywood film (*Finding Neverland*, 2004). The play itself has become the most successful children's play ever written. Certainly it is still one of few plays produced for children or families in the UK which is not based on a book or traditional tale, and among the most performed and well-known.

Peter Pan's long-lasting success does not mean the play is universally admired. It has been the subject of much debate, accused at various times of being imperialistic, misogynistic, twee, or even abusive. I do not aim to defend the play or its writer in this chapter, or to argue for or against the many opinions it has provoked. My interest is mainly in the way the story was created, through an adult playing with children, and how a large share of ideas at the heart of its enduring success came from those children themselves during that playing. In the last ten years I have taken this process as the starting point for a series of projects, and my purpose here is to explore the working methods and outcomes of those projects, creating plays for children by playing with children.

Analysis of *Peter Pan* often dwells on aspects of Barrie's own childhood and the psychological characteristics and regular preoccupations which find their way into the play. Although the evidence of his playing with the boys is acknowledged, the process tends to be seen as about a brilliant writer who is still stuck in his own childhood in some ways and is most at home with children, creating a world and a story for them (see Birkin, 1979; Chaney, 2005; Dudgeon, 2009). However, it has always been my understanding from the family story that this creative process was really much more collaborative than that.

The oldest three Llewelyn Davies boys first met Barrie in 1897, during their visits to Kensington Gardens, and it was through playing together with him and later with their two younger brothers that the story emerged. It is clear from their accounts that what they actually did was engage in a long process of what now might be called story-making: going on flights of fantasy, creating and enacting characters and taking them on various adventures. Barrie himself described the process later in a letter to the boys:

> I have no recollection of having written it. ... The play of Peter is streaky with you still, though none may see this save ourselves. ... As for myself, I suppose I always knew that I made Peter by rubbing the five of you violently together, as savages with two sticks produce a flame. That is all he is, the spark I got from you. (Barrie, 1924)

Barrie acknowledged that his job in writing the play was to select just a few of the many stories they had made up. As he wrote in an early version of the play's dedication to the boys, 'A hundred acts must be left out, and you were in them all' (Barrie, 1928; cited in Birkin, 1979:119). In the final version of the dedication he explained, 'You had played it until you tired of it, and tossed it in the air and gored it and left it derelict in the mud and went your way singing other songs; and then I stole it back and sewed some of the gory fragments together with a pen-nib' (Barrie, 1928; cited in Birkin, 1979:120).

The evidence of the children's creative role is strong in the play itself. In mixing together pirates, Cowboys and Indians, fairies, crocodiles and flying boys who never grow up, the world of Neverland takes the form of the world in which I have often seen children play, both in my own work and in my family. In my observation, children at play tend to move easily between worlds and mix the surreal, the mythical and the everyday, whereas most plays written by adults have greater internal logic. *Peter Pan* has the form and style of a play invented by imaginative and articulate children who were given the resources and license to play at will by the grown-up honorary child amongst them. That child no doubt enjoyed and celebrated their creativity and probably chipped in and developed ideas alongside them. The play has that form, I believe, because that is how it was created.

Furthermore, I am convinced that a big part of its success stems from this process, and that a significant reason it has always chimed so well with children and adults who like children, is that the best ideas, the spirit, the energy and the heart of the play all came directly from children at play. Even if it is felt that I am romantically exaggerating the role of these particular children in this particular play, it was my imagined version of the process which gave rise to questions: starting with a blank canvas, can we make up new plays for theatre companies to perform to children by playing with children? And if we do, what particular qualities will these plays have?

These questions grew alongside a series of developments in my own work. After ten years in a TiE team, Big Brum, which had inculcated in me a process of group devising through research, discussion and improvisation, I had evolved into a writer and director of professional theatre for young people. I was also doing regular freelance work making up drama with young people for them to perform themselves. I had begun to work with ever younger children, after I was involved in a major research project with under fives set up by Birmingham Education Department in 2002: *How to Catch a Moonbeam*.

This project, in which I was the drama worker, researched and explored the influential approach to early education pioneered by Loris Malaguzzi, in the northern Italian town of Reggio Emilia after which it is named. Reggio Emilia is a child-led and project-based approach, in which the arts, and professional artists in particular, have a distinctive role (see Edwards, 1993). Through this work I had experienced how the younger the children are the more the processes of drama and play converge. I began to do sessions where we would draw random objects out of a box and use them to trigger off stories. Evaluation of this process identified:

- an enhanced sense of enjoyment, fulfilment and engagement
- the development and valuing of creative and expressive skills
- the manipulation of ideas and feelings
- the development of language and communication skills
- the raising of personal morale, motivation, self-esteem and social development, and a positive feedback culture in which children felt encouraged and safe to take risks. (Pascal, 2004)

The responses of the children made it possible to attract support to take the work further, but the impact it had on me as a writer was also significant in suggesting possibilities which shaped the way the work developed.

I was already well advanced in this work, and aware of how much I enjoyed joining in with and scaffolding the creative play of young children, when the thought first occurred to me that this must have been what Barrie was doing in Kensington Gardens. As someone who struggles to make up stories, I recognised in myself the same delight he describes in the sheer flow and mixture of ideas from the very young children at play.

Here is an example. We were pretending in a nursery class one day that we were being chased by a tiger. So we needed somewhere to hide. But where? 'Let's go to Pizza Hut', a child said. 'Why?' 'Because in Pizza Hut there are toilets for boys and girls, but not for tigers.' It is brilliant: child logic, linking real experience and developing knowledge of the way the world works with the imaginary. Parents and early years workers will probably recognise inventiveness of this kind. To a playwright it represents a neat story idea that would probably never have sprung to the adult mind, and so presents fascinating possibilities.

In 2003 the opportunity arose to put these questions to the test when I was commissioned by Birmingham Repertory Theatre Company to write a play for children and involve pupils and teachers from five schools in the process. The model of work was in some ways set down for me, but within it we were able to work at some length with four classes of 6 to 7 year old pupils in primary schools and one special school group, with the brief of creating a play for full-scale production on the main stage based on their ideas. Classes of children were randomly selected from inner city schools, so the parallel with the privileged Davies boys taking time out of their daily walk in Kensington Gardens with their nanny was not immediately apparent. But the principle that guided the project was nevertheless a 'Peter Pan approach'.

The process was essentially simple. Firstly we needed to establish a feeling of playing, and get a creative flow started. This was achieved by being introduced to the class in role as Peter – a more forgetful and eccentric version of myself – who was trying to make up a play but clearly needed help. Peter was sitting on an interesting old box which turned out to be emotionally significant because it had belonged to his aunt who had come to England on the Kindertransport. It thus included the personal and the sad in our terms of reference, alongside the imaginary and exciting. The box was full of stories and things to do with stories.

The first thing to emerge from the box was a story book, but when we opened it we found that all the pages were blank. There was no story, something had happened to the story, we needed to find the story. Peter was a little desperate, and responded excitedly to any ideas that came from the group. Angela Lowry, one of the teachers involved in the project, described this stage:

> Peter listened to all the ideas, even the most bizarre. One child said, 'I'd like a colour blue story', another suggested 'a world without coats'. The children were able to replay these ideas in their imagination, often ordinarily dismissed by parents and professionals as nonsense. (Lowry, 2004:15)

By the end of the first session, we had established the process. The children had got the idea that the sessions would be playful but potentially emotional and serious, and that their imaginative contributions, whether verbal or physical, would be welcomed. One of the tasks of the teachers was to make notes of the ideas thrown out in sessions by the classes. A selection from those notes gives a picture of the content that gushed out:

> Burying the hamster... secret funeral ceremony
>
> Stepping stones
>
> Orange Zebra (not tiger)
>
> Surprises and sudden bangs
>
> You could put your head inside it
>
> As much popcorn as I like
>
> My cousin may be dead, he isn't in heaven or Wales, he is in Iraq
>
> All I would need is a bike my size
>
> The tiger can do anything, but only if someone wishes it. Everybody wishes for themselves, not for the tiger, so he is sad
>
> In the olden days people walked funny
>
> The tree house is dusty. There is a fire. We can get the birds to help us get down
>
> Or change the children into butterflies, and then change them back when they get down. (Wynne-Willson, 2004)

Seen in isolation as funny, sweet, fascinating things that children say, these examples show we were having fun; seen as ideas for a play they are gold-dust. What was evident from the very first session was that the need to make the play gave us a fine excuse and incentive for letting the children use their imagination freely for a while. The children were animated and produced idea after idea. From very early in the process they were committed to creating something special. With older children, this commitment might have stemmed from the perceived status of creating a play to be performed by professional actors on the main stage at the Rep but for these young children, most of whom had never seen a play in a theatre, this seemed to me to be more a reflection of the commitment and excitement they were picking up from the adults, plus the enjoyment they felt at being permitted to create a story on their own terms.

While much of the time at this stage was spent in discussion with the children, we also began to enact and make the ideas physical from early on. The ideas were often expressed physically, particularly with the less verbal groups, and as we moved on, using the box and objects, the ideas from one group were cross-fertilised with those of others. So a suggestion of stepping stones made by one group becomes flat stones in the box and the starting point for a drama session with the next group, and soon the stepping stones were common to all the groups, and no one remembered which group made the initial suggestion because we all owned them. One group invented the idea of a tree-house; a second spent time designing the tree house on paper; and a third built a tree house in the hall, so that together we could explore it and find out what might happen in it.

As the story came together, the sessions became more explicitly focused on the needs of the play. We spent individual sessions on the characters, the children being hot-seated in role or working in groups to draw up profiles. We brainstormed names: Iccy and Onga the twins, Mercedes the orange ladybird, the Foogle Peas and Stanley, the spider that is afraid of itself. In every session, and in response to every question, out poured ideas that I felt were effortlessly more interesting than I could have arrived at alone.

Of course 125 children cannot write a play, and the job of putting these ideas into a workable shape fell on me. However, we began to find that if the process remained obsessively committed to ensuring the play came from the children, they could be involved with many of the key decisions, even around structure. My instincts as writer constantly informed my choice of which elements to pursue, so I tended to respond positively to suggestions that seemed helpful to the structure that was developing in my head. However, I tried to remain open to other options as long as I could and often found that although I was expecting the story to go a certain way, a more interesting alternative would arise from the children.

The importance of remaining open in terms of the direction of the story was illustrated quite late in the process. We had a great deal of the story in place, and I was anxious to find a reason for why our baddie, a park keeper called Bradley, was so determined to keep children away from his park, or what we called The Shooky. So I brought this issue to the children. I expected that we would find some story from Bradley's childhood, and I led the exploration of this. Some of the suggestions were good: that he was angry because so many people broke the rules; that he was picked on when he was little; or that his mum had died. None of these seemed to satisfy the children, and although I tried not to show it, I was becoming concerned. Then someone said: 'I know. He has had a spell put on him by a witch.'

I was caught up in my adult quest for psychological truth, and took the idea without finding it helpful. But the little girl persisted, and I remembered in time to stay open to possibilities and in the end this became the explanation adopted. Later literary analysis of the story might raise the question of whether the spell cast on Bradley had a psychological significance – but it had emerged as a child's pragmatic answer to why Bradley was like he was. For 5 or 6 year olds, the supernatural may help explain what is hard to understand in the world. Allowing children to participate in the creation of a story is not just a lesson in trusting the value of their reasoning and their explanations of the world around them, it also demonstrates how stories provide stepping-stones to understanding human behaviour or exploring it through archetypes and symbolism. Imposing a psychological reason that makes sense to an adult may confuse children, spoiling the story and the way it operates on the level of a child. Realising this made the process intensely exciting.

With the resources of Birmingham Rep main stage and production departments, as well as a strong director, designer and six actors, the later stages of the process rewarded the children's creativity. They attended rehearsals, briefed the actors on their parts and made inputs into the design, costume and even the marketing of the play. Most striking about this stage was the confidence the children had in their own work and their strength of ownership. One teacher observed:

> They really loved it as their nonsense ideas were beginning to make sense, and they were committed to paper, programmes and then the stage. They had such energy for the play, they felt it belonged to them. (Wynne-Willson, 2004)

The Shooky was duly performed to audiences of the same age as the creative groups or a little older. Angela Lowry described her group attending:

> The children felt it was all there because of them, they had made it happen. Four year groups from my school went to see the performance and were still talking about it at the end of term. Children were playing games about it in the playground and trying to make stepping stones to get to Tiger Island. I truly believe there is immense value in using their imaginative ideas in such a fantastic way that boosts their morale and makes them want to write. (Lowry, 2004:15)

I was very keen to develop the approach further, and seized the opportunity presented by a commission from Moby Duck Theatre Company in 2005 to write a play on a Korean theme for a national tour to 'family audiences'. I encouraged the company to let me create a new story, using a development of the *Peter Pan* approach, and we embarked on the project that became *Horangi Yohaeng*, or *Tiger Trail*. This was set up differently – there were only two groups of children and they were younger. One group was a reception class in Wolverhampton of 4 to 5 year olds, the other a kindergarten group in Seoul, South Korea, of 5 to 6 year olds. This time the final play would be restricted to three performers and had to be suitable for touring. However, the principle would remain the same: creating a play through playing with children.

The starting point was broadly the same as for *The Shooky*. The story box with the empty story book and the need to find a story were presented to each group, and a relationship, playful atmosphere and creative flow were established. The obvious difference was that the two groups were 6000 miles apart so were linked differently. I was able to start both projects in person, but after my initial session in Korea the group continued to play with a Korean colleague, Kim Sori, while I remained in the UK, playing with the Wolverhampton reception class, the 'Rascals'.

Despite seemingly huge differences, the process was remarkably similar. The ideas were shared through emails, images and videos, which we found in the box at each session. As the two groups did not share a language, and perhaps because they were so young, the exchange was more physical. But we again followed a pattern from the big explosion of initial ideas, through the cross-fertilisation between the groups, into narrowing in on the needs of the play – characters, settings and story structure. Again we enacted as a group, and hot-seated the characters. These children were the youngest I had tried this with and I was surprised at how well they jumped into it. Again my notebook reveals the tell-tale signs of children's imaginative play – the mixing of the imaginary and the mundane:

> Socks the tiger
>
> Meeting a lizard – he goes from Birmingham to Pakistan
>
> In a boat to the Post office, with David Beckham
>
> Chido is very interested because we found out her name means 'map' in Korean
>
> A black hole necklace which sucks everything in... (Wynne-Willson, 2006)

The two groups could have had only sketchy ideas about each other. Before I went to Korea I asked the Rascals what I should take and they suggested pictures of cars and televisions and computers to show the Korean children what they were like. However both groups of children responded readily to the ideas generated by the other. Moreover, they shared more cultural references than we might have expected thanks to Disney and Harry Potter. The play was certainly gaining from the breadth of cultural references. Tigers, lizards and volcanoes, which meant more in Korea, were welcomed into the UK story alongside the bin man and the footballer.

As with *The Shooky*, the sense of ownership was impressively equal in both groups. Each felt they had made up the whole story, and that was fundamentally true. Later in the process, Sori arrived in the UK to act in the play and came out of the box at the start of a session, much to the Rascals' surprise. The Wolverhampton group was again fully involved in the production stage of the play, working with the actors, attending rehearsals and correcting whatever they felt had been misunderstood. The scale was much smaller and the production itself never got to Korea, so the Korean group built their story towards a performance which they did for parents, and watched the UK production on video.

The variety and mixture of creative ideas covered in the final performance of *Tiger Trail* provided powerful evidence of how the play had been created. When writing plays for a young audience, the received wisdom tends to be that 'less is more' and that a good production will have simplicity as well as depth. But when children make up stories or older children write them they generally move swiftly from one episode to another which often is seen as a flaw in the play and a sign of inexperience of writing. I do not disagree with this view, so remained anxious that we should have narrowed down to make the play feel somehow neater, more manageable and more satisfyingly complete. I attributed the great number and flow of ideas to the number of children, not just their age.

But during the process it became clear that this was my adult preoccupation, and not the way the Rascals wanted to go. So I tried to resist the temptation to make the story neat for myself and the other grown-ups. However, it is true to say that I did not succeed completely, and although I did not impose adult logic on the play, I did lead the group a little at the final stages of decision-making and influenced the resolution of the story. Loose ends were tied, and although the final play was extremely well received by young audiences, I wondered whether that adult neatening had saved the play from being too messy and confused, or had damaged its child-logic and spirit.

So when I used the *Peter Pan* approach in a third project, I resolved to be braver about avoiding imposing adult logic. The Playmakers Project was commissioned by Birmingham Rep and Birmingham Family Learning Service to create a play by working with young children and their families. It led to the development of the most ambitious play to date *Princess and Ginger* (2007). It worked with even younger children and spread the creation part of the project over two terms. The five groups involved were four nursery groups aged 3 and 4, and one group of 2 year olds. Each group was relatively small, with only eight to ten children participating. For the first time parents were included in each group. Although this clearly took us some way from the original *Peter Pan* model, it offered an opportunity to engage parents and take the story-making process into the home.

The starting point remained the box and the blank story book. Again working across the groups, the parents took on the role of idea-catchers. Their task was to note in some way the story ideas that came from their children, both within the sessions and during the week between each session. The adults were instructed to avoid leading or influencing these ideas. Many parents found this interesting and valuable and said they enjoyed their role as idea-catchers and that they were seeing a different side of their children. But for me the main excitement of this project sprang from the young age of the participants and my increasing confidence about allowing the final play to have a structure that truly reflected the wishes of the children who made it. By now I had learned to recognise when a grown-up impulse was rising and to try and resist it.

If you trust children to decide things, you are constantly surprised by the decisions they make. Such young children may lack an understanding of the needs of theatre, but they also lack the preconceptions that sometimes help, but more often restrict, our imaginations. For example, when we played out the story during the later stages of the creation of *Princess and Ginger*, the children wanted to repeat elements more frequently than I would have done, and this time they shaped the play structure – against my adult playwright instincts.

In performance in nurseries and early years settings, the rhythm of the play was at times quite slow and repetitive, but though this was indeed criticised by some adults, it appeared to be appreciated and understood by the children in the audience. The play was strongly reminiscent of the children's creative play from which it sprang, and there seemed consequently to be an invisible line that linked the play's creators with the children watching the performance.

These three projects were all fascinating and enjoyable in their own right, and the impact on the children involved in each case was powerful and positive. Evaluation of the projects showed a strong sense of ownership of the final performance and their sense of achievement for their own part in it. They also gained in confidence, communication and self-expression, as well as learning specific creative skills. The impact on the artists, teachers and, in the final project, the parents and carers, was also marked. At the *Charting Antarctica* conference organised by Birmingham Repertory Theatre in 2008, the parents and children made a presentation about the process to an audience of artists and educators. The project was partly funded by Birmingham's Family Learning Service and was targeted specifically at parents who had left school without qualifications. Yet at the end of the process the group of parents made a clear contribution to a potentially intimidating gathering. It was an eloquent demonstration of their level of commitment to the project and the confidence they had gained through it.

The value of these processes to those involved was sufficient to justify them and to persuade me to encourage others to set up similar approaches to playing and plays. But they also generated plays which had a particular quality that made them unusual. I do not want to over-stress the *Peter Pan* connection, as we moved far from anything that happened in Kensington Gardens in 1900. We have not created a new *Peter Pan*; none of these plays have been picked up by Disney, nor will they be funding Great Ormond Street Hospital for years to come. However they did share the sense of fun that ensues from joining in with children at play, and the delight that comes from trusting young children as the creators of theatre. I am sure many writers spend time doing this anyway, but I will continue to encourage people to take it that bit further, and I hope to have many more chances to see just where the world's young children can take me to in future.

References

Barrie, J M (1901) *Peter Pan*. London: Hodder and Stoughton

Barrie, J M (1924) Dedication to Peter Pan Unpublished. Copyright Great Ormond Street Hospital

Birkin, A (1979) *J M Barrie and the Lost Boys*. London: Constable

Chaney, L (2005) *Hide-and-Seek With Angels*. London: Hutchinson

Dudgeon, P (2009) *Captivated*. London: Vintage.

Edwards, C (1993) *The Hundred Languages of Children Westport*. Connecticut: Ablex Publishing Corporation

Lowry, A (2004) *Child Education*. Leamington Spa: Scholastic

Pascal, C and Bertram, T, Bokhari, S, Burns, P, O'Neill and Young, S (2004) *'How to Catch a Moonbeam and Pin It Down' Project Interim Research Report*. Centre for Research in Early Childhood

Wynne-Willson, P (2004) The Shooky, Unpublished notes and play script, performed by Birmingham Repertory Theatre Company

Wynne-Willson, P (2006) Horangi Yohaeng or Tiger Trail, Unpublished notes and play script, performed by Moby Duck Theatre Company

Wynne-Willson, P (2007) Princess and Ginger, Unpublished notes and play script, performed by Birmingham Repertory Theatre Company

6

Creating theatre work for a
diverse teenage audience

Dominic Hingorani

Introduction

As Chris Elwell, director of The Half Moon Young People's Theatre recognises, making work for teenagers is 'not a genre with a coherent identity or boundaries' (2010) since teenagers may as likely be an audience for and enjoy adult work and vice versa. However, it is clear that teenage audiences, increasingly autonomous in their cultural consumption, are amongst the hardest to reach and engage with for theatre makers, especially outside the confines of the classroom. In a digitally saturated culture, many young people may have little direct experience of live theatre and may find it irrelevant. In this chapter, I explore how engaging with this challenge in relation to teenagers has led to innovation in practice and form and the creation of relevant, serious and emotionally challenging theatre work. This is focused specifically on work that addresses the diverse ethnicity in the teenage population of East London. I will look at three cases studies: *Mad Blud* (2008) at Theatre Royal Stratford East; the *Exchange For Change* (EFC) programme at Half Moon Young People's Theatre (2009-2011); and *Guantanamo Boy* (2012), at Stratford Circus Arts Centre.

Ethnic diversity, teenagers and the arts

In 2009, Arts Council England noted its concerns about an imbalance between ethnic groups in engagement with the arts:

> the level of parental encouragement differs by family background and personal
> demographics: parents of high social status are more likely to encourage their

children to engage in the arts; girls and white children are more likely to receive encouragement than boys and children who are not white. (Oskala *et al*, 2009: 2)

In the East London boroughs of Newham and Tower Hamlets, in which Theatre Royal Stratford East, Stratford Circus and Half Moon Young People's Theatre are located, over 50 per cent of the population belong to an ethnic group other than white British and the proportion of young people is higher than the national average . Both groups have historically low levels of engagement in the arts. As the McMasters report noted, 'we live in one of the most diverse cultures the world has ever seen, yet this is not reflected in the culture we produce, or in who is producing it' (2008:11). Consequently I examine models of theatre praxis which aim to address issues of diversity and representation in the creation of work for young audiences. So I have chosen three examples of practice that positively take account of, rather than disavow, the diverse ethnicities of the population in which they are located in East London and operate through a range of strategies which include the following: policies on representation and casting, subject matter, source material, methodological approach, modes of engagement and audience development.

Mad Blud – A London Story: authenticity and representation

In 2008 Theatre Royal Stratford East initiated a verbatim theatre project, *Mad Blud*, in response to the marked rise in knife crime in the borough which particularly affected the teenage constituent of their audience. In this respect, *Mad Blud* adhered to the theatre's long-standing artistic philosophy of 'the continuous loop' that, as Artistic Director Kerry Michaels explains in interview:

> picks up on the aspirations and concerns of the community ... we put those on-stage, and the people with those aspirations and concerns see the work, which feeds into the next show and even into the dialogue of the show itself. (2011)

Using this approach, *Mad Blud* sought to engage a primarily teenage audience with the serious issue of knife crime and related gang culture. The demographic imperative of this objective is clear: Newham has one of the youngest populations in the UK with 68 per cent of residents aged under 25. With 180 languages spoken, it is one of the most diverse boroughs in the country. I discuss the efficacy of this and assess how *Mad Blud* attempts to intervene in the politics of representation and contest discriminatory discourses that operate around issues of race and criminality, especially concerning knife crime.

The project began in the spring of 2008 as a result of initial discussions between writer/director Philip Osment and Theatre Royal. The aim was to develop a piece of verbatim theatre on the subject of knife crime. Osment initially envisaged that the piece would revolve around a single incident. He would interview family, friends, teachers, social workers and the perpetrator involved in the incident, which he soon realised was 'all completely unrealistic, as I found, as you are dealing with people's grief and people's pain' (2011). Instead, he initiated a verbatim theatre project in which multiple viewpoints and experiences were presented.

One problematic area was gaining access to, and achieving the trust of young people to get them to share their experiences and responses to such a sensitive issue in order to develop the verbatim text. To address this problem a core team of eight investigative journalists was formed to collect testimonies from the existing network of Theatre Royal community contacts. Drawing members of the outreach team from the community and having them initiate contact gave the team the methodological advantage of being able to engage with families and victims of knife crime in a way that members of a theatre could not.

In the first phase, the investigative reporters recorded testimonies from relatives, friends, neighbours and even people on the street in an attempt to gather an authentic response to the community's experience of knife crime. This first incarnation of *Mad Blud* toured secondary schools and pupil referral units in the borough as well as Theatre Royal, in order to get feedback from their core constituent. A key aim of this project was not only to represent the marginal voices of young people in relation to this issue but also to engage their response to it.

The benefits of the verbatim form were noted by a reviewer at the scratch performance of *Mad Blud* in July 2008 who recognised that 'the impact of the work comes much more from the knowledge that these are real voices being given a public hearing' (Loxton, 2008). The piece was fifty minutes long and represented a range of voices including teenagers talking about gangs and knife crime in relation to the black community, first generation immigrants from the Caribbean, a police officer describing a knife crime and the response and a mother whose daughter has been stabbed. Notably, there was no material from a perpetrator of knife crime at this first stage.

In October 2010 *Mad Blud* developed further with the circulation of an advertisement asking the community once again to engage with the project. The scope now extended beyond engaging young people as interviewees and audience members, as six outreach workers, mainly young people, were recruited and trained to conduct the interviews. The stories featured in the subsequent 2011 production included those of:

- a perpetrator: a black teenager who has been in prison for stabbing another over a turf war
- the family of a teenager who was stabbed and killed who are struggling to cope with the death, how it happened and the poor treatment they felt they received from the police and hospital
- a mother whose daughter had been killed by a school friend
- a young adult who was assaulted but reconciled with the perpetrator
- three elder women of Caribbean origin outside a church who were discussing the lack of accountability in the local community and the lack of respect for adults shown by young people today
- a range of local public opinions on why knife crime is increasing.

Eliciting multiple viewpoints and narratives from a range of interviewees, the company adopted the approach to verbatim pioneered by Alecky Blythe and her company Recorded Delivery, whose work draws on communities responding to events. The conversations recorded were not only one-to-one but also took place between groups of people. At the heart of the performance of this material is the technique of unlearnt delivery: rather than listening to and learning the scripts of the interviews and then performing the characters, the actors do not learn the lines and are instead fed the text through headsets during the performance. As they hear the text, the actors repeat it as accurately as possible to let it remain as unmediated as possible. Though this is intended to lend authenticity to the text, with its hesitancies, colloquialisms and non-sequiturs, the technique foregrounds the gap between actor and character.

The play opened with all five actors arranged on a traverse stage, counting to three and pressing play on their MP3 players which were connected to visible headphones. The audience was also played an excerpt of what the actors were listening to, to frame the concept of the recorded delivery performance. While the productions give the audience an insight into a range of perspectives on the issue, including, tellingly, that of a perpetrator in the 2011 production, the material remains open and without editorial, to allow them to engage with the complexity of the issue. Director Osment was quite clear that 'I don't have the answer [so] post show discussion was about the audience talking to each other' (2011). In this respect the audience responded both to the verbatim form and hearing real voices onstage as they engaged with those involved on the inside rather than with how the issue was represented, especially by the media, from the outside.

As with all verbatim and documentary work (Hammond and Steward, 2008; Forsyth and Megson, 2009), artistic choices had to be made to shape the material and decide which voices were included and excluded. The guiding principle was to highlight the impact knife crime has on the diverse groups within the community by including conflicting and contrasting viewpoints which presented the issue's complexity. An epic theatre approach also enabled actors to play multiple roles in the production so that the voices were not cast by type or ethnicity. A scene in which a young white male actor played the older black women of Caribbean origin who were attending church created a hugely comic effect, for example. This approach to integrated casting was facilitated, with the proviso that the overall cast contains a spectrum of ethnicities that reflects the diversity of the verbatim material gathered.

Featuring such a range of voices enabled Mad Blud to represent the variation and complexity inherent in the black community's response to, and experience of, knife crime as victims, concerned citizens and, at times, perpetrators. As one critic recognised, 'the play was successful in dispelling common stereotypes by pointing out that knife crime is not exclusively an issue for the Black community' (Bhuiyan, 2011). *Mad Blud* placed the experience and response of teenagers centre stage and demonstrated a praxis model whereby difficult cultural and social issues, such as knife crime, gang culture and 'black on black' crime could be discussed without didacticism or a simplification of the issues. In this respect *Mad Blud* was a methodological success because it created a space where the performance provoked dialogue amongst the audience members.

Exchange for Change: Half Moon Young People's Theatre
The aim of the Half Moon Young People's Theatre's innovative EFC programme, a three-year art form development project, was to develop 'new artists and new plays for young people which reflect the diversity of our community' (2011). Each year of the programme focused on creating work for a different age range: Year one for under 7s; Year two for teenagers; and Year three for 8 to 12 year olds. The Half Moon is based in the diverse community of Tower Hamlets and the EFC initiative had an explicitly interventionist agenda to offer 'developmental opportunities for artists who are currently under represented in the sector in terms of ability (disability) or cultural diversity' (2010:3). The programme also wanted to encourage established writers to

write for young audiences and create challenging and relevant productions for the theatre.

EFC was based upon a successful new writing collaborative project, Wild Lunch Funsize, between Half Moon and new writing company Paines Plough in 2008. During the project six plays for children under 8 were developed with experienced writers who were writing for a young audience for the first time. EFC continued its strategy of engaging 'experienced writers to write for young audiences for the first time' (2010:3) and also developed the programme to address interdiscipinarity alongside diversity by including artists from a range of art forms and disciplines. The theatre used a dual strategy to develop emerging practitioners, who are often from ethnic minority backgrounds, and allowed them to work collaboratively across a range of art forms. Practitioners from more traditional disciplines such as dance, theatre and stage design worked alongside a digital media artist, an MC, and a lyricist, whose work is particularly immediate for, and popular with, the teenage audience.

Artists were encouraged to adopt an interdisciplinary approach through exercises in the initial workshop. Many did not have experience of a theatre rehearsal room, so the process included early sessions facilitated by the directors at the Half Moon which introduced the devising process. Artists within the groups reported that they didn't have pre-existing rehearsal methodologies to share and that they used instead a process of trial and error.

A key plank of the methodology was for the groups to participate in facilitated workshops with the target age group as part of the six development days scheduled for each ensemble. These two encounter sessions were structured to occur near the beginning and end of the process and were intended to be an opportunity for the groups to share the work in progress and develop key themes with the participating teenage audience. The pieces created by the end of the process were given work-in-progress performances or rehearsed readings. These were showcased at an annual one day festival accompanied by discussions with an invited audience of professionals working with young people or engaged in producing theatre work for young audiences.

Three ensembles devised and showcased in the second year of EFC, producing *Glass Knickers*, *Frag-mENTAL* and *The Closer I Get the Distant I Am*. *Glass Knickers* explored ideas of gender and stereotype through dance, digital art and text, in collaboration with school groups aged 12 and 13. Following discussions of what might constitute the ideal boy or girl, the piece examined such serious themes as the objectification and representation of women within the context of young people's relationships. It was a vital element of

64

the process that the young people involved in the collaboration through the encounter sessions felt free to speak honestly and openly. This allowed the adults making the work to ensure that it was recognised by the audience as both representative of their experience and relevant.

I would like to look in more detail at the process of the group who created *The Closer I Get the Distant I Am*, a physical theatre piece which looked at how young people communicate and touched on the issue of self-harm. The ensemble was made up of black, Asian and white performers, including Vipul Bhatti, a contemporary dance artist who specialises in the Indian dance form of Kathak, Nick Tyson, a jazz musician and Tamsin Kayembe aka Concise One, a lyricist/MC. In the development process the group was comfortable to share and explore each other's disciplines, something that was exemplified in the performance in which the lyricist and musician danced and the dancer and musician also performed the spoken word. The form not only permitted inter-disciplinary experimentation, it also allowed an innovative performative collage of dance, spoken word and music that dramatised both the literal and psychological space of the character to emerge.

Ironically, a key theme incorporated in the final work came as a result of the artists' difficulty in engaging the young people at the first encounter session. As they were constantly referring to their mobile phones, all the characters in *The Closer...* were plugged in to either a mobile phone, an MP3 player or a computer, which illustrated the importance of digital media in young people's lives. In one scene, for example, two girls who are best friends sit side by side on a bench but converse via text messages displayed on the projection screen during the performance.

Lyricist Tamsin Kayembe played the main protagonist, a young black woman who is navigating and negotiating her relationships at home and friendships outside. While the subject matter of boyfriends and best friends is understandably staple fare for this age group, the central character is not afraid to make challenging observations in relation to her cultural context, such as 'my cousins are having babies and some of them are still babies' (Half Moon Theatre, 2010a:6). This emphasises the authenticity of the context. The following description of home food extends this concern to the representation of ethnicity:

> pickles and Chuck-Ney
> biriyani
> dumplings
> mutton curry

koeksisters

coconut ice

boerevors

cool aid

coconut slice

(Half Moon Theatre, 2010a:6)

It is the EFC imperative set out in the evaluation report – and exemplified by the encounter sessions – to 'creat[e] new work through the involvement of the target audience' (2010b:3) that in no small part gives it the methodological confidence to do so.

Guantanamo Boy: bridging the gap between literature and theatre

To address the recognised shortage of emotionally challenging theatre work for teenage audiences, Stratford Circus Arts Centre commissioned Brolly Productions in 2009 to create and produce a stage adaptation of *Guantanamo Boy*, Anne Perera's critically acclaimed novel for teenagers. Here, literary adaptation became both a source of other, often untold stories from minority communities, and addressed the questions posed by Claire Connor, director of Stratford Circus: 'how [do]... we tell our young people about the very worst that we are capable of as human beings? How [do] ... you responsibly help them to understand the world they live in?' (2011)

Guantanamo Boy 'pulls no punches in its depiction of the torture, isolation and injustices suffered by prisoners at the notorious camp' (Pauli, 2009) and the central character Khalid, a Northern teenage British Asian boy. At the heart of the novel is Perera's concern about the transgression of human rights in the context of 9/11. The book responds to the reports including those by human rights organisation Reprieve that over twenty children under the age of 16 have been held at Guantanamo Bay since it has been opened in 2002 (Reprieve, 2012).

This particular adaptation provided an opportunity to develop a teenage audience new to theatre by building a methodological bridge between contemporary fiction and theatre. Central to this enterprise was the organisation of the *Performing Human Rights Symposium* (2011) which became a key part of the development process in the making the adaptation. After initial discussions between the novelist, commissioning venue and theatre makers, an agreement was reached for the project to proceed and artistic freedom was granted to Brolly Productions to create the stage adaptation. The novelist did, crucially, remain in the development process, attending rehearsals, work in progress performances and, specifically, speaking at such events as the symposium.

The symposium created a day-long forum for an invited audience of young people from a range of local and national constituencies. It included a performing arts group from a Newham secondary school, a reading group from Newham Bookshop, representatives from Youth Amnesty, Penguin Books' youth readers group Spinebreakers, the Muslim Women's Writers group and other minority community organisations. It also included a number of theatre professionals and arts organisations.

The young people were invited to watch a 20-minute work-in-progress of the stage adaptation of *Guantanamo Boy* and participate in a workshop which explored the creative process of adaptation. They also engaged in discussions about the wider issues raised in relation to the transgression of human rights, representation and minority communities and the geopolitical context explored in the novel. These discussions were led, alongside Brolly Productions and the commissioning team at Stratford Circus, by the novelist Anna Perera, representatives of the Human Rights Lawyers' Association and Amnesty.

The symposium provided both a space for young people to engage with and respond to the issues raised in the novel and an opportunity to give developmental feedback to the work-in-progress. It therefore facilitated a wider dialogue amongst the young audience and developed their relationship with the project and the production. The symposium operated as a model for a local engagement of the teenage audience and fulfilled the aim of both the novelist and adaptors of the play to encourage young people to discuss the issues raised by 9/11 and the long-term fear and paranoia it provoked. It might also serve as a model for how to develop a new theatre audience.

Conclusion

The productions discussed in this chapter clearly recognise that as for an adult audience, the issue of diversity is not only a key imperative in the development of a representative teenage audience, it is also inextricably linked with the creative practice. My discussion of diversity has narrowly focused on ethnicity and cultural identity, but its implications can extend to disability, sexuality and beyond. The approaches I have discussed have begun to apply a range of strategies which creatively engage with other, often theatrically marginalised, voices. It is clear from the examples that such engagement provokes innovation in practice. That might be in form, as exemplified in the verbatim or interdisciplinary practice discussed in relation to *Mad Blud*, or it might be in the active and meaningful engagement of young people in the process of making and shaping the work. It is hoped that this will lead to the development of a teenage audience that is not only representative of the culturally rich and diverse communities that make up contemporary Britain but also acts as a catalyst for creative theatre practice.

References

Bhuiyan, A (2011) Review of *Mad Blud* at Theatre Royal Stratford East Studio. http://www.ayounger theatre.com/review-mad-blud-a-london-story-stratford-east-theatre May 2011

Connor, C (June 2011) Interview with author. Performing Human rights Symposium Stratford Circus Arts Centre

Elwell, C (2010) 'Foreword' *Exchange For Change Programme*. Half Moon Young People's Theatre Archive

Forsyth, A and Megson, C (2009) *Get Real: documentary theatre past and present*. Basingstoke: Palgrave Macmillan

Guantanamo Boy (2012) adapted and directed by Dominic Hingorani. Stratford Circus, London 31 January-11 February

Half Moon Theatre (2010a) The Closer I Get The Distant I Am. Unpublished play text.

Half Moon Theatre (2010b) Exchange for Change Year 2 – Teenagers. Unpublished External Evaluation report, Half Moon Young People' Theatre Archive

Half Moon Theatre (2011) *Exchange For Change*. http://www.halfmoon.org.uk/theatreprofes sionals/exchangeforchange.htm October 2011

Hammond, W and Steward, D (eds) (2008) *Verbatim Verbatim: Techniques in Contemporary Documentary Theatre*. London: Oberon

Loxton, H (2008) Review of *Mad Blud* (Scratch Performance). http://www.britishtheatreguide. info/reviews/madblud-rev.htm October 2011

Mad Blud (2008) by Philip Osment, directed by Dawn Reid. Theatre Royal Stratford East 18-29 February

McMasters, B (2008) *Supporting Excellence In The Arts: from measurement to judgement*. London: Department of Culture, Media, Sport and the Arts. http://webarchive.nationalarchives.gov. uk/+/http://www.culture.gov.uk/reference_library/publications/3577.aspx September 2011

Michaels, K (2011) Interview with author

Oskala, A *et al* (2009) *Encourage children today to build audiences for tomorrow*. London: Arts Council England

Osment, P (June 2011) Interview with author. For Evaluation of *Mad Blud: A London Story*. Theatre Royal Stratford East

Pauli, M (March 2009) Guantanamo for kids. *The Guardian*. http://www.guardian.co.uk/books/ 2009/mar/03/anna-perera-guantanamo-boy September 2011

Performing Human Rights Symposium (2011) Stratford Circus, 9 June

Reprieve (2012) *Reprieve*. http://www.reprieve.org.uk/ March 2012

7

Intercultural performances for young audiences in the UK: engaging with the child in a globalised society

Karian Schuitema

This chapter deals with the possibilities of intercultural performances as ways of engaging with the child's experience of contemporary globalised society. Children's theatre opens up possibilities to represent and engage with an interconnected world and diverse society, rather than reducing discussion about globalised society and intercultural performance to how global economics oppresses and standardises local cultures. While acknowledging the problematics of intercultural production, the chapter examines how placing the child at the centre of the theatrical experience and, importantly, the creative process preceding the production can engage young spectators at both global and local levels and at the same time allow them to become active participants in a global cultural exchange.

The connective processes of globalisation are changing the lives of children in the UK. A majority of children now live in cities where migration and immigration have significantly altered and diversified the ethnic and cultural make-up of society (Madge, 2001:20-4). At the same time, British society is globally connected through terrestrially broadcast, web-based and digital media. Cheap international air-travel is increasingly available and purchasing products and food from all over the world is now the norm. First, second and third generation children of those originally immigrating to the UK are likely to stay in touch with family and friends from the cultures or family networks they left, using these forms of media, communication and travel (Vertovec, 2009). Such global connectedness increases the child's exposure to cultural differences and contributes to an awareness of the world as a single, although varied, place. Although these contemporary realities are broadly recognised to have an impact on the lives of children, the concept of globalisation is often, particularly in the area of theatre studies, associated with the arts becoming increasingly commodified through free-market economies and the ever-growing power of multinational companies (Bharucha, 1993; Wickstrom, 1999; Rebellato, 2009; Harvie, 2004). Some commentators fear that a Western capitalist monoculture will eventually devour and destroy all local and minority cultures (Lechner and Boli, 2005:140).

Although much children's theatre reflects on the child's experience of a globalised society by staging and exploring different cultures as well as stories set or originating elsewhere in the world, a contradiction is frequently created. On the one hand, globalisation is interpreted by practitioners and critics as a wholly negative macro-economic concept and process; on the other, it is deemed important that the child engages and reflects on their place in a global society. Globalisation is a term and a process that encompasses more than economics, and a restricted economic discussion will not benefit children's theatre. Robertson for example, argues that globalisation is the growing interconnectedness of the world and the resulting awareness that the world can be seen as a single place (1992:8). He points out that globalisation is a cultural process which is interpreted differently in different places, and suggests that far from being the opposite of each other, the global and local are in continuous interplay, what he calls 'glocalization' (2007:546-7).

To discuss how theatre for children can engage and facilitate engagement not only with the growing interconnectedness of the world but also with what should be avoided when addressing cultural difference, I examine two case studies: *The Lion King* (1999), a musical aimed primarily at young children and *Once Upon A Tiger* (2010), an international production for young audiences. I use *The Lion King* to discuss the negative effects of the global market structure and the dangers of an intercultural performance that exploits cultures. My discussion of *Once Upon A Tiger* is presented as an example of how to engage with a young audience on both global and local levels at the same time. It also shows how the creative process can use the connective processes of a global world and provide the child with an opportunity to explore cultural differences.

Intercultural performances

According to Knowles, intercultural performances can function as 'sites of negotiation' that evoke 'the possibility of interaction across a multiplicity of cultural positionings, avoiding binary codings' (2010:4). The intercultural performance can create a theatrical dialogue where different cultural references and practices are performed together to create a cultural mix or hybrid forms. This might include performances and stories told with Indonesian Shadow puppetry, African drums and other performative elements taken from a specific culture that are performed in productions with a different cultural origin. In many instances there will be a writer, director or performer from a certain cultural background who creates these performances with an integral knowledge of the culture to which they belong. In other cases, performances might have been created through cultural exchanges or collaborations between two or more countries.

The intercultural nature of a performance is also established through an exchange with the young audience. It is only through the audience's active interpretation of the performance text that meaning is constructed so understanding the frame of reference through which every young audience member approaches a performance is essential (Schuitema, 2009). Such a frame of reference is constructed through previous and direct experiences which makes the child's local environment and cultural background integral to the way they perceive theatre. Even when a performance is only representative of a single culture, the diversity of both the audience and their interpretation, shaped by their frame of reference, ensures that the intercultural dialogue is nonetheless established. As the UK is a culturally diverse society, a certain level of this intercultural exchange is inevitable.

Alongside governmental advice and pressure groups such as Platform for Intercultural Europe, theatre practitioners frequently argue that intercultural projects can help bridge gaps between cultures, encourage understanding and promote equality, as well as represent and empower cultural minorities living in the UK (Frank, 2008). Interculturalism is a contested term and practice, however, one that evokes many problems in Western societies with colonial pasts and neo-colonial presents. It raises many questions about the homogeneous, exploitative and unequal powers that underline all intercultural exchanges (Stone Peters, 1995:205).

It is not possible to provide the full extent of the intercultural debate in the space of this chapter, but with the emphasis on globalisation it is important to note that intercultural production is frequently seen as a Western phenomenon that appropriates and re-negotiates cultural difference to suit the needs of the market. Bharucha argues that Western intercultural performances are potentially 'involved in the draining of source cultures through arbitrary, non-negotiated, and essentially one-sided modes of transportation determined by the globalising mechanisms and complicities of the market and the state' (1997:32). Bharucha and others characterise current intercultural practices as forms of Orientalism (Said, 1978). Bharucha argues that the Western practice of interculturalism is not a cultural exchange, instead 'it is the West that extends its domination to cultural matters' (Bharucha, 1993:2). Although Bharucha writes mainly about how cultures in his native India are affected by Western global powers, his criticism can extend to all the countries which, in his terms, belong to the Third World. Disney's *The Lion King* has been chosen an example of an intercultural performance which is engaged in this globalising mechanism.

The Lion King

The Lion King premiered in Minnesota on 31 July 1997 and opened at London's Lyceum Theatre in 1999. The musical was adapted by Elton John, Tim Rice, Hans Zimmer, Lebo M and director Julie Taymor from the animated Disney film of 1994. Featuring a young lion cub named Simba who is in line to the throne of the Savannah, the film was already part of a global brand. The stage production had to find a way to transfer the animals to the stage and represent the African setting of the story. Its creators embraced the challenge by incorporating various performative elements that the West typically associates with African culture: costumes made out of fabric with West African wax prints, music with rhythmical Conga drums, masks resembling traditional African wooden masks and water urns, the set with earthy natural colours, and a selection of dance from tribal rituals (Disney, 2011). The show is set in the African savannah with African animals, and in its African setting it celebrated and reproduced an essentialised representation that elided the cultural diversity of a whole continent within a Western theatrical form.

Julie Taymor argues that the musical's global success is rooted in its universal appeal, as the themes of the story, such as father/son relationships and the balance of nature, in addition to the intercultural performative elements, are recognisable anywhere in the world (Disney, 2011). However it could be argued that notions of African cultures are selected and appropriated to sell in the West and its universal appeal functions as a homogeneous and standardising force within the market structure of capitalism.

The musical also represents the danger of the arts and commerce merging, creating a phenomenon that Wickstrom calls 'retail theatre'. Wickstrom points out that advertisements in the programme of *The Lion King* tells audience members to 'enjoy your audience with the King. And remember, even in the jungle, American Express helps you do more' (1999:285). This advert, she argues, not only illustrates how theatre and the market have become entwined, but places and inscribes the audience in the fiction of the musical by suggesting that they are also in the jungle and are having an audience with the King (1999:285). The commercial reason for placing the audience within the fantasy world of the play rests on the idea that the consumer wants to buy the experience (1999:297-8). As Wickstrom writes:

> By creating environments and narratives through which spectators/consumers are interpellated into fictions produced by and marketed in both shows and stores, entertainment and retail based corporations allow bodies to inhabit commodities and so suggest that commodities, in turn, can be brought to life (1999:285).

The African setting of *The Lion King* functions simultaneously as a set for the global market and, by commodifying the experience as well as the characters and the world they inhabit, it enables the Western audience to buy and consume a Westernised version of African culture. As a consequence *The Lion King* becomes a global product: culturally representative of no-one but equally consumable by everyone, or at least those for whom economic considerations do not bar access.

Rebellato discusses this type of 'retail theatre' and its usage of the global market in his book *Theatre & Globalisation* (2009). He groups successful global musicals under the term 'McTheatre' as they operate under the same standardising principles which aim to provide the customer with the same 'quality' experience anywhere in the world (2009:41). The fantastical world of *The Lion King* has been transported and subsequently staged in fifteen different countries, where each performance featured identical replicas of the masks and sets (Disney, 2011). According to Rebellato mega musicals turn the theatrical performance into a standardised franchise which limits the liveness, uniqueness, and immediate experience of the audience, as the individual performances can no longer connect to space and time (2009:41-2).

To return to Bharucha's criticism of the intercultural performance, in the case of *The Lion King* the creative process is underlined by the capitalist appropriation of cultural specificity. In this process, the show exploits features of the source culture to generate profit for the producers of the show. Nothing is given back to the source culture. However, it is important to address the limitations of such a model of cultural production. The capitalist appropriation involved in the creative process does not mean that spectators at *The Lion King* engage in a homogenised theatrical experience. Such a view undermines the role and participation of the audience and suggests that the spectator, instead of actively constructing meaning, only consumes in a passive sense. It appears that the audiences' engagement in Wickstrom's retail theatre is limited to buying the ticket or paying to be part of the fiction and experience.

Such criticisms also assume a monolithic audience that will interpret and understand the performance according to the same frame of reference, rather than acknowledging the cultural diversity that can be found in the UK. The argument that *The Lion King* has taken the local cultural specificities of the African continent and shaped them into a standardised global product, which is the same anywhere in the world, has to consider that this global product needs to be interpreted on the local level of the audience, and, to complicate matters further, a local level which is interpenetrated by the global.

The interaction between the local and global levels, which occurs when an audience enjoys a theatrical performance, relates to Robertson's concept of 'glocalisation'. It is partly attributable to the impossibility of separating the child's experience and interpretation from their immediate environment and culture, including, for example, the building, the journey to the theatre and even the person they sit next to. Despite Rebellato's assertion that *The Lion King* is no more than a global standardised and homogenised theatrical experience, the same anywhere in the world, the child's visit to the mega musical remains an individual experience, formed by the perception and connection they have to their direct environment and informed by their cultural background. The global world of the stage is therefore interpreted in relation to the child's local environment, which is influenced in turn by the global interconnectedness of society.

The interaction bears many similarities to the intercultural production which features a dialogue between the culture performed on stage and the culture of the receptive audience. Although I have argued that *The Lion King* resituates aspects of African culture in the format of a Western musical, some of these cultural elements are clearly recognisable for their cultural difference, such as the music created by the South African musician Lebo M, whose compositions use African languages like Zulu, Xhosa and Swahili. This influence proved too culturally different for some critics, who argued that one of the problems of the musical is the fact that the songs are unmemorable (Dalglish, 1999; Elkin, 2004; Cavendish, 2009).

A child with a South African background living in the UK may interact with these elements in a completely different manner to a child with a different background, and might perhaps enjoy the cultural representation. Moreover, the cultural elements shaped more profoundly by Western consumer culture will also contribute to the intercultural interaction. Although multinationals like Disney and McDonalds are deemed to represent a global culture consumable by all, many individuals in the West do not feel represented by this consumer culture and choose to reject these particular influences. If we consider such different levels of engagement and differences in interpretations, it is useful to reject the notion of a single global culture and instead regard these as competing cultures that use the global market for their efficient spread around the world (Hopper, 2008:109). In this consideration, the staging of one of these competing global cultures still establishes some form of intercultural dialogue with the audience.

Although *The Lion King* has the potential to provoke an intercultural dialogue and, unlike a standardised global product, has possibilities to engage with its audience on both a global and local scales it is important to recognise that Bharucha's criticism that intercultural performances use cultural appropriation in their creative process is not addressed in this discussion. Such appropriation is not wholly due to the 'globalising mechanism' but rather to the capitalist structure that underlines the process of the cultural exchange. The cultural exchange is motivated therefore by the commercial appeal of the cultural other. The second performance discussed in this chapter, a small-scale subsidised project called *Once Upon A Tiger*, is an example of a completely different interpretation of the intercultural exchange.

Once Upon A Tiger

Once Upon A Tiger by Moby Duck was established through collaboration between two groups of children: one from the UK who live near Birmingham and another from the outskirts of Seoul, South Korea. The project used a specifically designed blog which allowed them to share ideas, learn and engage with each other's culture, despite their geographical distance. The project's designer Peter Wynne-Willson ultimately wrote the final script with contributions from Yoon Won Hye, developing the storyline from various suggestions made by the children. Wynne-Willson also directed the production with professional actors. It toured the UK in 2010.

The participating children decided to set the story in South Korea because the title, *Once Upon A Tiger*, as well as being a sentence found at the beginning of many traditional stories in South Korea, was the only pre-established element of the play. South Korea is a country with which the UK has had no direct history of colonial involvement, nor can it be described as a 'Third World country', the term Bharucha uses to theorise the flow of cultures. However,

Asiatic countries such as South Korea and Japan are part of the 'Orient' as constructed by Western cultures. Western intercultural productions that represent these particular cultures still risk presenting this 'Other' through stereotypes or solely in a historical context, rather than with an awareness and appreciation of the contemporary culture. Such problems routinely arise, for example, by using stage make-up to accentuate stereotypical physical properties such as yellow skin; rendering English dialogue in pidgin form or with exaggerated accents; portraying the Oriental character as less intelligent than their Western counterparts; or, using costumes to suggest that everyone in Asiatic countries is dressed in kimonos, wears conical straw hats and uses handheld fans.

The project blog for *Once Upon a Tiger* shows how the two groups of children took inspiration from their immediate environments and personal concerns when devising the play. At the same time, each thought about and engaged with the culture of the other participants. The creative process of *Once Upon A Tiger* provided the participating children with an opportunity to get involved in an intercultural exchange; one that took place on both local and global scales simultaneously.

An early contribution by the South Korean children was to set the play around an old local tree (*once upon a tiger,* 2009). The children wondered how it had survived the Korean War fifty years earlier, and the English group were asked if they were aware of this war. The South Korean children decided that as it was so special to them the locals had protected it during the war with arms. They also discussed what their town looked like 700-800 years ago.

The South Korean children uploaded multiple pictures of the tree onto the blog which allowed the English children to continue the discussions concerning trees, war and the past. The English children tried to find explanations for why a tree would be so important to the people of a town or village and came up with the following reasons: the tree held happy memories; it was a repository for secrets; there was a myth that if the tree were to fall down it would be the end of the village. The children also wanted to share their favourite tree in England: a conker or horse-chestnut tree. The introduction of a red squirrel, which one English child had seen on a tree, ultimately became the play's highlight: an out-of-tune singing squirrel who lives in the ancient tree.

The final script charts an inventive and creative story, incorporating several original ideas that included a flying tiger rug with fitted pizza oven. The story follows Young Hee, a brave, energetic, technology-loving girl and her nervous friend Andy Sherbert, as they journey to understand a grumpy old lady,

Charlotte, and learn the secrets of her tiger rug and the old tree in her garden. The play text was a result of the intercultural exchange, facilitated by the web-based and digital media that in contemporary society interpenetrates the child's direct environment with global influences.

The challenge for the performance was to re-establish such a dialogue with an audience who were not involved in its creative processes. Even though the children had sent pictures of some of the costumes and staging, the director still had to decide how the cultural influences would be represented in the play. The play did not seek to present an historical Oriental representation to reinforce the South Korean setting, but it was not devoid of cultural references either. One of the three performers was South Korean and delivered her lines in Korean throughout. Her performance was made understandable by physical gestures and through the interaction with the other characters. The music accompanying the play was mainly Western, but a gong and rhythmic drumming related to forms such as P'ungmul, the Korean drumming and dance tradition, were also incorporated.

In contrast to *The Lion King*, these cultural references were not selected and adapted to sell in the West. It is impossible to claim that *Once Upon a Tiger* existed outside the UK's capitalist market structure and I would not argue that participating in the intercultural exchange without the motivation of maximising profit wholly negotiates the problems and criticism of the intercultural production. However, the small scale of the performance changed the dynamics of the exchange. For example, in small productions staged in smaller theatre venues, the relation between performance and audience is much more intimate (Way, 1981:65). Small theatre spaces literally bring the audience closer to the performers and their actions. This arguably encourages children to feel more involved in the action of the play and this is further stimulated by audience interaction or participatory elements (Way, 1981). Such proximity and interaction, which may neither be invited nor an official part of the performance but rather a spontaneous incident initiated by the child, produces the need to re-establish the spectator-performance relationship each time a production is staged so that every performance becomes unique.

In *Once Upon a Tiger* planned audience interaction occurs when a hunter attempts to shoot the tiger and asks the audience for advice on the angle from which to aim. At performances I attended some of the audience members reacted by discouraging the hunter while others gave genuine advice on the best way to kill the animal. The moment of interaction might only be brief but it increases the audience's presence within the performance and thus the intercultural exchange. Furthermore, this presence allows the local scale, the interpretation of the play according to the child's space, time and frame of reference, to interact with the global influence of the play and *vice versa*. If we consider that the local scale of the child is interpenetrated by the global influences of society, and the local interpenetrates the global influences of the play in the active participation of the children in the creative process, *Once Upon A Tiger* illustrates a full interaction of the global and local scales.

Conclusion

In demonstrating the interaction between the local and global scales, *Once Upon a Tiger* challenges the dominant proposition that globalisation is wholly an economic process in which a standardised global culture oppresses local cultures and reduces the interactivity of the theatrical event to a consumerist transaction. While the discussion of *The Lion King* shows that although the play's creative process and cultural engagement are compromised by its cultural appropriation, the audience interaction and participation in the intercultural dialogue cannot be assumed to have been standardised and homogenised. By contrasting the hugely profitable international musical with a small-scale subsidised production, I have argued that the absence of a primarily commercial motivation increases the possibilities for the intercultural interaction. Placing the child, not profit, at the centre of the creative processes allowed participants in the creative process of *Once Upon a Tiger* to engage in an authentic exchange between cultures using contemporary technology that increases global interconnectivity. In performance, the small scale brought performers and audiences closer and increases the interaction between both cultures and the global and local scales that interpenetrate the performance as well as the audience. The girl who wrote in the blog that 'hopefully our play will become famous in the worldwide' seemingly understands the global scale of the project (*once upon a tiger*, 2009). She is an example of a generation that looks beyond the national borders of the UK and for whom the theatre needs to engage with an interconnected and diverse society.

References

Bharucha, R (1993) *Theatre and the World: Performance and the Politics of Culture.* London: Routledge

Bharucha, R (1997) Negotiating the 'river': intercultural interactions and interventions. *TDR* 41(3) p31-8

Cavendish, D (2009) *The Telegraph. The Lion King* at the Lyceum Theatre, review. http://www.telegraph.co.uk/culture/6375768/The-Lion-King-at-the-Lyceum-Theatre-review.html February 2011

Dalglish, D (1999) *London Theatre Guide-Online. The Lion King*, review. http://www.londontheatre.co.uk/londontheatre/reviews/lionking99.htm February 2011

Disney, *Exploring The Lion King.* http://www.exploringthelionking.co.uk February 2011

Elkin, S (2004) *The Stage. The Lion King*, review. http://www.thestage.co.uk/reviews/review.php/2405/the-lion-king February 2011

Frank, S (ed) (2008) *The Rainbow Paper. Intercultural Dialogue: From Practice to Policy and Back.* Brussels: Platform for Intercultural Europe

Harvie, J (2004) *Staging the Nation.* Manchester: Manchester UP

Hopper, P (2008) *Understanding Cultural Globalisation.* Malden and Cambridge: Polity Press

Knowles, R (2010) *Theatre & Interculturalism.* Basingstoke: Palgrave Macmillan

Lechner, F J and Boli, J (2005) *World Culture, Origins and Consequences.* Oxford: Blackwell Publishing

Madge, N (2001) *Understanding Difference: The meaning of ethnicity for young lives.* London: National Children's Bureau

once upon a tiger (2009) http://onceuponatiger.blogspot.com October 2010

Rebellato, D (2009) *Theatre & Globalisation.* Basingstoke: Palgrave Macmillan

Robertson, R (1992) Globalisation, Social Theory and Global Culture. London: Sage Publications

Robertson, R and Aart Scholte, J (eds) (2007) *Encyclopedia of Globalisation.* Volume Two. London: Routledge

Said, E W (1978) *Orientalism.* London: Routledge and Kegan Paul

Schuitema, K (2010) The possibility of an intercultural children's theatre in Britain. In J Plastow and M Hillel (eds) *The Sands of Time.* Hatfield: University of Hertfordshire Press

Stone Peters, J (1995) Intercultural performance, theatre anthropology, and the imperialist critique: identities, inheritance, and neo-orthodoxies. In J E Gainor, (ed) *Imperialism and Theatre.* London: Routledge

Vertovec, S (2009) *Transnationalism.* New York: Routledge

Way, B (1981) *Audience Participation.* Boston: Walter H. Baker

Wickstrom, M (1999) Commodities, mimesis and *The Lion King*: retail theatre for the 1990s. *Theatre Journal* 51(3) p285-98

8

White Peacock: a play for audiences with complex disabilities: rising to the challenge of Article 31

Gill Brigg

Introduction

Article 31 of the UN Convention on the Rights of the Child states that: every child has the right to rest and leisure, to engage in play and recreational activities appropriate to the age of the child and to participate freely in cultural life and the arts (1989). Polly is a 15 year old labelled as having profound, multiple and complex learning disabilities (PMLD), for whom the full attainment of Article 31 is extremely challenging. She is described as having a range of sensory impairments, arrested intellectual development, along with a number of physical conditions which mean she uses a wheelchair. Some art forms are available to her; she loves listening and dancing to music – heavy rock in particular. She is a lively participant in school performances alongside her friends, and interacts with IT software to create digital art.

The focus of my research, and this chapter, is the creation of specialist theatre work for audience members like Polly, who are seldom seen at public performances and for whom specialist theatre is rarely created. I maintain that Polly, like everyone else, should have access to theatre in the form of an emotionally rich fictional experience created through the symbiotic relationship between suspended disbelief, allowing the 'as if' to occur while creating the 'aesthetic distance' established by theatre conventions (Schonmann, 2006: 66). I am specifically interested in the way an aestheticised experience presented through the theatre elements of light, sound and action can engage Polly in the performance but at the same time protect her from mistaking fiction for reality. In June 2010, Polly and her classmates were part of my doctoral research project which culminated in a piece of new theatre writing, *White Peacock*, created with the needs of audiences with PMLD at its core (Brigg, 2010). I wished to create an opportunity for such audiences to participate in theatre according to the aforementioned parameters and to work closely with them in the process.

The challenges to accessing theatre

It is likely that Polly's capacity to access theatre is connected to the cognitive and sensory challenges which limit her capacity to recognise the culturality of theatre spaces, the plays they contain and the social behaviour expected within them. Susan Bennett usefully defines this cultural phenomenon as an interrelated system of frameworks:

> The outer frame contains all those cultural elements which create and inform the theatrical event. The inner frame contains the dramatic production in a particular playing space. The audience's role is carried out within these two frames and, perhaps most importantly, at their points of intersection. (1997:139)

Bennett presupposes that audiences are able to understand the function of such frameworks and so can access the events that happen within them. Polly's access to the cultural concept, space and pretence associated with theatre demands bold and sensitive examination.

The reason why Polly has been denied access to this cultural construct rests on the centrality of the verb 'to understand' in Western culture. My experience of working in this field has led me to think that the challenge for Article 31 lies not with the nature of the audience but rather with the nature of theatre-making itself. Most theatre Polly might encounter requires her to engage her brain to understand both the content of the play and its cultural construct. This is fundamentally a cognitive activity and within it lies objective understanding. Polly, however, requires embodied not embrained activity to reach a state of understanding appropriate to her cognitive capacity, so a theatre experience needs to reach her through alternative and multiple sensory channels. I believe it might be possible to create a new performance lexicon which explores audience reception from this exciting and creative perspective. I examine this idea with reference to *White Peacock*.

Only when the unique qualities of her atypical body are accommodated will Polly be able to access all the components of the theatre experience. She has occasionally visited the theatre alongside her parents, and together they have been required to become resourceful adventurers embarking on an experience fraught with systemic barriers. Moreover, Polly is impeded in her access to buildings, auditoria and facilities. Problems arise if another wheelchair user also needs access, as even in these relatively enlightened times of disability discrimination legislation in the UK, generally only one wheelchair at a time can access lifts and there is little space to park adapted vehicles close enough. Staff in the building seldom have adequate training in how to support audience members with complex needs. For example, logistical support is required to attend to personal care needs in a fifteen minute interval.

In addition to her own needs, Polly has to contend with how her fellow theatregoers react to her 'otherness'. Other members of an audience may be unable to disattend Polly's communication behaviours because they have no experience of sharing social and cultural space (Elam, 1980:88). Richard Manners describes the issue:

> Some people with learning difficulties exhibit behaviour which we may find strange, but it is actually our inability to recognize these behaviours as valid and acceptable which further alienates the individual with learning difficulties from the community. (1998:511)

Polly could thus become part of the performance. Her presence causes the experienced theatregoer to swiftly re-draw their 'horizon of expectations' based on a performance situation characterised by stillness, quiet and external audience passivity (Jauss, 1982:20). These challenges are heightened when Polly visits the theatre as part of her peer group with similar needs. Societal norms encourage people with learning disabilities to partake in cultural consumption in groups. This makes the problem more acute, with facilities in most arts venues simply incapable of adequate access provision. Even if Polly can sit in the auditorium alongside other theatregoers, the distance between the performing area and where she is seated is likely to be too great for her, given her sensory impairments, to engage with the performance. The show simply does not reach her and she remains a passive witness to an activity that happens somewhere beyond her perception.

Creating the frames in *White Peacock*

To address these issues, *White Peacock* was performed within a purpose-built micro-theatre erected in Polly's familiar school hall. It was made to accommodate another five classmates, each of whom brought a companion. The micro-theatre contained a full lighting rig, sound system and a series of tracks and curtains which could hide and reveal designed elements within the play. Polly could choose where to sit throughout the piece and was encouraged to enter and return to the space whenever she chose. Two permanently open entrances and assistance from her companion facilitated this. Free traffic was an important function of the micro-theatre and briefing the companions to enable Polly's choice of vantage point was key. As Tony Jackson writes about Theatre-in-Education: 'there are perhaps few worse experiences in this field of work than to find oneself belittled or one's dignity undermined within a supposedly participatory event from which there is no escape' (2007:8).

The cultural outer frame was constructed in the classroom in advance of the play. Meanwhile, the teachers worked through the preparatory tasks in the teachers' pack to introduce key words about the theatre conventions and also the plot. On the morning of the performance the actors generated anticipation through song and story-telling. Care and time were taken to create an appropriate horizon of expectation by gently nurturing the audience's curiosity. Polly was moved towards an understanding that an event was about to take place. The journey of the audience from the classroom to the micro-theatre, in pursuit of the musician playing the accordion, was a crucial part of the construction of the outer frame, as they joined in the anticipation that a story about a white peacock was going to happen in a theatre in their hall.

Once inside the micro-theatre, Polly was invited to access *White Peacock* via the performance signing systems of light, sound and action and thus enter Bennett's inner frame. I was aware that the moment when the outer frame acquiesced to the inner frame, when the real world became the fictional world, was a time when Polly would be particularly vulnerable. For example, in theatre buildings the need for the audience to focus on a represented reality is often signalled by a change of lighting. Shifra Schonmann believes that this moment of interface needs to be handled with particular care for new young audiences who may be prone to fear (2006:90). This is especially important for audiences with PMLD .

In Western culture today, the non-disabled theatregoer is likely to have a horizon of expectations which includes being aware of the need to diminish noise, settle into a comfortable position, cease interaction with others and await the gradual disappearance of existing surroundings. For many spectators, the dimming lights herald a portentous moment, rich with expectation, but for Polly it is just getting dark slowly. While the rest of the audience waits in hushed anticipation for the fiction to start, Polly may feel she is just sitting in a quiet room. She experiences what Roland Barthes calls 'innocence', while surrounded by experienced theatregoers who can fluently interpret the signification contained within the changing environment (1975:120). Furthermore, as the interaction with her companion diminishes as she attempts to conform to accepted notions of a quiet audience, a feeling of solitude and a breaking of connection with the external world can prove stressful. Polly may be anxious about what is going to happen in the quiet darkness and may require verbal or tactile reassurance by her companion.

Once the performance is under way Polly may not have the cultural history to understand signification systems nor the neurotypical filters which allow her to disattend stimuli which are extraneous to the piece. These might include the emergency exit signs, the stage manager entering the space to re-configure the scenery or the perfume of the woman sitting nearby. I therefore felt it was important for Polly's initiation into the inner frame that careful attention was paid to the moment of transition. Having settled within the micro-theatre, Polly was encouraged by the performing team to interact with her companion as much as she needed to for reassurance and clarification. Schonmann, in her discussion of first time young audiences, writes of a young woman wanting 'to be sure that [the adults] were there with her' (2006: 77) and stresses the importance of adult support in anchoring children safely in the real world whilst they explore the fictional world (2006:79).

As well as providing companion support for Polly, the company all welcomed her specifically, singing her name in a composition in which the harmonic and rhythmic complexity steadily grew. As the central character began to speak in role to her and her classmates, the light state within the micro-theatre began to change exceedingly gradually. Within fifteen minutes, Polly had entered a theatre space, been connected to a supportive and known companion and experienced signification elements of the inner frame. Her initiation had begun and she was ready for the story.

Narrative concerns

White Peacock is a story about a young disabled man called Sam, who is going through the transition into adulthood. Throughout the play, written in close consultation with Polly's school, Sam faces challenges which lead him to the ultimate goal of his first kiss. The play is structured to enable the audience to experience key narrative moments across the time span of a single night in the young man's life. These moments exist as stand-alone events, each containing a different emotional mood which is communicated through a range of senses.

Polly's school encouraged me to write a piece that would explore her life experiences. She is a young woman in the midst of adolescence, experiencing sexual awareness and about to begin the journey towards independence from her parents, so these issues became the themes of the play. Schonmann's analysis of the processes a child undergoes whilst experiencing theatre centres on catharsis. She cites a number of applications of this term, many of which audiences with PMLD will find cognitively challenging, such as the capacity to link together events in a play in order to have an emotional connection with it (2006:71).

Schonmann views catharsis as 'supporting one's emotional life, and helping a person to function better outside the walls of the theatre' (2006:71). This view of catharsis inspired me to give *White Peacock* its emotionally intense landscape. As both a teacher and writer, I sense an assumption that young people with PMLD are perceived as needing *protection* from difficult emotions. It is assumed that they might not understand these emotions, or could find them upsetting or hyper-stimulating. The case study below reveals otherwise.

TYA and sensory stimulation

Perhaps this is why most theatre companies who specialise in performance for people like Polly focus predominantly on sensory stimulation and not on inherently dramatic narratives which might challenge the emotions. I have learnt a great deal from these companies over the years but wanted to provide Polly with an initiation into a theatre form that combined what I had learnt about sensory approaches with an emotional dimension. To define theatre as a sense experience is to take away the need for meaning to be cognitively constructed as well as sensed. The theatre company Oily Cart, for example, is exemplary in the way they follow a micro-theatre approach within which to serve the senses of their audience with PMLD. Theatre is served as a palette upon which the five senses can be sampled in a physically comfortable and flexible environment in which the sensory discourse flourishes. In addition to the common acoustic and visual channels of theatre signification, touch, smell and taste are key components in their work. In *Conference of the Birds* (2005) large fans made of giant leaves provided not only a rich tactile stimulus but also a source of gentle breezes. Bamboozle's residencies in collaboration with the National Theatre's production of *War Horse* in 2007 used a puppet which, as Christopher Davies recounts: 'neighs, whinnies and snorts and blows through its nostrils, which creates great excitement when the children feel the warm air' (2009:14).

The sense of smell is a key access point for Polly. Writing about the importance of aroma in aesthetic understanding, Yi-Fu Tuan notes that 'smell, compared with sight and hearing, affects our emotions at a more deeply buried level. The olfactory sense is linked to the primitive part of the brain that controls emotions and mood' (1993:125). This suggests that emotions can be triggered directly without conscious cognitive processes taking place. The use of aroma in the work of theatre companies who work with disabled audiences such as Oily Cart, Bamboozle and Interplay is well established. They recognise that smell is 'more intertwined in emotions than any of the other senses' which makes it a valuable channel of communication for Polly (Chu and Downes, 2000:112). I argue that it is possible to create active emotional spectatorship for Polly through the use of the sensorium which enables her to engage with theatre in a way that had been largely denied to her.

The greatest responsibility I felt towards Polly was to provide her with a clear distinction between fantasy and reality so she could have a safe and comfortable journey through the experience. Although 'sad' moments in performance may *feel* sad they are only *fictitiously* sad. Schonmann insists that 'the child's awareness that the play is fiction must be ensured' (2006:67) and I wanted to guarantee that the inner frame signalled an unmistakably fictitious experience. For example, the moment the main character kissed his friend was repeated three times, with progressively increasing emotional intensity, so it was firmly placed in the fictional and not the real world. Such moments cannot be replayed in real life.

Through the clear and bold multivalent configuration of light, sound effects and music, I hoped Polly could begin to understand that these sad, happy or troubling moments were not real since moments of this nature are not accompanied in real life by sudden changes of lighting and a crescendo of music. To further support the clarity of the reality/fiction binary, Polly would need to be given clear signposting towards important emotional moments within the play and sufficient time to process it. Lighting and music (or indeed silence) helped foreground such moments and support her focus. Some of her classmates are hearing or visually impaired, so a range of technical enhancements, as well as tactile stimuli, were used to heighten impact. An example of this was when Sam discovers that his favourite tree has been blown down in a storm, a tree in which the peacock had built its roost. The peacock is an important part of Sam's life and it has disappeared. He discovers this loss with his new-found friend Phoebe:

Sam: He's gone and my tree's gone.

(Sam picks up a pile of sticks and snaps them)

Sam: (in between snapping sticks): Cracked. Broken. Snapped. Twisted. Crunched. Smashed. Damaged. Dead. My tree.

(Sam cries within a tightly spotlit area. After a few moments of his crying amidst silence, the 'sad' musical theme is gradually introduced.)

(Phoebe moves around the space signing 'sad' and directing attention to sad Sam. If and when the audience signs back or makes eye contact with her, she affirms their reaction with a sad expression or nod of her head. The audience is offered the opportunity to handle and snap sticks or to touch the sticks Sam has already snapped.)

Although Schonmann takes the view that 'emotional tension in theatre for young people should be of shorter duration than for adults' (2006:83), this need for emotional clarity means that such moments must be elongated for Polly and made deeper and clearer (2006:83). Schonmann's concern is that the child may become so deeply engrossed in the intensity of the emotion that they are unable to maintain aesthetic distance and believe it to be real (2006:65). But I suggest that by using the devices of light, sound, music and repetition, this distance is still maintained and the fiction reinforced.

Seeing *White Peacock* twice in a single morning with only a half hour break between performances may well have done most to reinforce for Polly that the drama was fiction. I decided to do this on the premise that seeing it twice over would significantly increase the maintenance of aesthetic distance because real life does not happen twice. The first performance would fulfil an initiatory function into the outer and inner frames and the second would enable Polly to relax and enjoy the emotionality of the play.

The capacity of the actors to occupy a liminality between the world of the audience and the world of the fiction was key to Polly's access. Their skill lay in being able to calibrate the intensity of the experience within the inner frame so as not to unsettle or overstimulate her. This liminality allowed them to mediate between the audience members and the play, sometimes encouraging focus from the strength of their work within the scripted world of the fiction, sometimes from the threshold of the fiction and reality – as the aforementioned Phoebe – and sometimes from 'real' interactive sensory work with Polly on a 1:1 basis. The following example from the script illustrates the latter:

Change of LX to light the whole space.

The formality of the performance space dissipates as the two actors encourage the audience to explore and choose activities. There is [musical] underscoring with Garden Wash theme.

Activities:

Exploring the pond: putting feet in the water, looking at the submerged lights, touching the wet stones in and out of the water, feeling the contrasting textures in and around the pond, sitting on the grass bank.

Exploring the reed screen: following a green torch beam which Sam shines through the screen, touching the texture of the screen with hands, feet or faces, peeping at someone on the other side of the screen, hiding.

Exploring strips of turf taken from the base of the grassy mound: placing the turf under cheeks, hands, heads, feet, touching the muddy side of the turf, smelling and tasting the grass.

Exploring a basket of herbs: tasting, feeling and smelling a range of seasonal herbs.

There should be a sense of discovery and spontaneity. The activities are carried out with sensitive negotiation. Wherever possible attention is paid to preference and choice.

The work of actors

As references to *White Peacock* within this chapter show, working with Polly and her classmates places huge demands on actors. Those who have experience of Theatre-in-Education are often skilled at working with liminality and facilitation but have rarely operated the three-way communication required to link themselves to Polly and her companion. This triad works most effectively if a range of communication systems are used, including speech, PECS symbols (Picture Exchange Communication System) and Makaton (a system using signs and symbols). The process requires sensitivity and skill to encourage openness and trust so Polly's communication remains the focus of the actors.

When working with profoundly disabled audiences actors are required to steer a safe course through the play, 'reading' their audience continuously without patronising or rushing them. In this case, they needed to challenge Polly to access the narrative through her own choices and not through a potentially disempowering series of instructions. In rehearsals for *White Peacock* it was helpful to offer the actors some training in Intensive Interaction, a method of communication originally developed by Phoebe Caldwell for working with autistic young people (2007). Her system of mirroring unique sounds and actions helped them understand how Polly might indicate her sensory preferences through her own communication systems (Zeedyk, 2008). Tim Webb, artistic director of Oily Cart warns of the need to be vigilant across all communication channels:

> It can be difficult with particular individuals to interpret their body language and other ways of communication. A twist of the head can be a way of indicating delight, and another's way of communicating apprehension. So the performers have to remain aware of the companion's responses. (2005:198)

Webb alludes here to the state of awareness required whilst performing for audiences with PMLD. Unlike the usual relation between performers and spectators, it is crucial that the actors actively watch the audience – not the other way round.

Conclusion

Gathering evidence within such a project is fraught with ethical and practical challenges. It entails complex navigation of safeguarding protocols, the protection of choice, and parental permission. I gathered phenomenological evidence over a period of a year through video recording and interviews with students, teachers and companions. How, then, can I prove that Polly was able to engage safely with the emotionality of *White Peacock*? The most useful evidence was gathered during the two performances attended by Polly and her classmates. Polly did seem to be engaged in the narrative and was able to access the emotionality of the plot as was corroborated both by video and an interview with her companion. I asked Polly's companion how she knew that engagement had taken place and she replied: 'Polly the whole time was watching and was engaging with it. [She] was engaged the whole time and stayed in that space. If she wasn't we would have been out of that door.' A teacher working in the class noted that all of the students were significantly more engaged during the second performance. She felt the repetition enabled one young man in particular to find the courage to enter the space and engage willingly with the emotionality of the plot, despite the anxiety that had prevented him doing so during the first performance.

The evidence showed clearly the audience's enjoyment of the rich emotional landscape, which highlights educational and developmental benefits in addition. The emphasis on personal choice enabled by the visible exits in the micro-theatre, alongside the range of sensory activities offered in the performance, was seen as extremely empowering for Polly and other traditionally disenfranchised people.

Throughout my time working in this field I have heard consistently positive feedback from young people with PMLD, via their companions or advocates, teachers and family members. They recognise the value in creating specialist pieces. Disability discrimination legislation for inclusivity guarantees physical access to theatre, although with only limited capacity. But exclusive custom-built theatre enables pieces to be created which are appropriate to Polly's age and designed to accommodate her specific learning needs. The development of a more extensive body of knowledge on the application and efficacy of the kinds of practices outlined in this chapter can only assist in securing access to the rights enshrined in Article 31 for audiences with PMLD.

References

Barthes, R (1975) S/Z, trans. R Miller. London: Jonathan Cape

Bennett, S (1997) *Theatre Audiences: a theory of production and reception.* London: Routledge

Brigg, G (2010) Theatre for audiences with profound and multiple learning disabilities: addressing and assessing access to performance. Unpublished PhD thesis, University of Nottingham and Nottingham Playhouse

Caldwell, P (2007) *From Isolation to Intimacy: making friends without words.* London: Jessica Kingsley

Conference of the Birds (2005) written and directed by T Webb. Oily Cart, remounted tour. June 2005

Davies, C (2009) Multi-Sensory Theatre. Bamboozle Blog. http://www.bamboozletheatre.co.uk/multi-sensory-theatre. September 2009

Chu, S and Downes, J (2000) Odor-evoked autobiographical memories: psychological investigations of Proustian phenomena. *Chemical Senses* 29 p111-16

Elam, K (1980) *The Semiotics of Theatre and Drama.* London: Methuen

European Convention on the Rights of the Child. Article 31. http://www.unicef.org/rightsite March 2011

Jackson, T (2007) *Theatre, Education and the Making of Meanings: art or instrument.* Manchester: Manchester UP

Jauss, H R (1982) *Toward an Aesthetic of Reception.* trans. T. Bahti, Minneapolis: University of Minnesota Press

Manners, R (1998) A Personal Journey: drawing on difference. In Rees, M (ed) *Art Therapy with People who Have Learning Difficulties.* London: Routledge

Schonmann, S (2006) *Theatre as a Medium for Children and Young People: images and observations.* Dordrecht: Springer

Tuan, Yi-Fu (1993) Passing strange and wonderful: aesthetics, nature and culture. In A Lepecki and S Banes (ed) *The Senses in Performance.* New York: Routledge

Webb, T (2005) Special needs audiences. In S Bennett (ed) *Theatre for Children and Young People: 50 years of professional theatre in the UK.* Chippenham: Aurora Metro Publications

Zeedyk, S (2008) *Promoting Social Interaction for Individuals with Communicative Impairments: making contact.* London: Jessica Kingsley

9

Impossible audiences: The Oily Cart's theatre for infants, people with complex learning disabilities and other young audiences who are primarily non-verbal

Tim Webb

Introduction

How do you make theatre for people who are unable to see or to hear what is happening on stage? How do you put on shows for people who become very anxious when encountering new people or situations? How do you create performances for people who may not understand that this is a story and that the actors are pretending to be other people? Why would someone who cannot recall what happened 30 minutes ago want to sit through an hour-long play? How do you create theatre for people who do not use verbal language? These are some of the questions that this chapter addresses with reference to the work of Oily Cart over the past 30 years.

Oily Cart and early years audiences

Oily Cart is a theatre company based in London that was formed in 1981 by the designer Claire de Loon, musical director Max Reinhardt, and myself as writer and director. The three of us continue to originate the productions of the company to this day. Claire has had a considerable career as a theatre designer, including two years with the Glasgow Citizens, as well as with fringe and Theatre in Education companies. She has also worked in extensively in community and youth education. Max Reinhardt has had a great deal of experience as a teacher, including several years as head of the Family Workshop at Battersea Arts Centre. He has a substantial reputation as a world music DJ and is one of the regular presenters of BBC Radio 3's *Late Junction*. I began working as performer and writer with the TiE teams at Glasgow Citizens and in Greenwich, and spent two years as assistant director at the New Victoria Theatre in Stoke-on-Trent. The three of us came together when we were all working at Battersea Arts Centre and decided that we would like to create a show for 3 to 5 year olds. Inspired by the work of a pioneering young people's theatre company called Theatre Kit, one of the first in this country to take performance for children under 5 seriously, we made our first show, *Out Of Their Tree* (1981).

At this time, 1981-82, most of our fellow professionals considered children under the age of 5 an impossible audience because of their limited attention span. However, there were party entertainers who would take on audiences of any age with a few magic tricks, a little puppetry, some sing-alongs and balloon modelling. At the same time, both the TiE teams with which I had been involved had tried productions for these very young children. On the whole, theatre professionals avoided these audiences, perceiving them as having limited language skills and an inability to sit still.

However, beginning with *Out Of Their Tree*, we found we could communicate effectively with under fives so long as our shows used themes, language and characters accessible to the very young and employed a wide and regularly changing variety of theatrical languages, including strong visuals and live music. Our early scripts took as their starting point a setting or situation likely to be familiar to our audience: *Out Of Their Tree* was set on and around a battered old tree in an inner city park; *Bedtime Story* (1983) was based on the process of going to bed. We would always depart from these everyday settings, however, and spiral off into fantasy, hoping that our initial approach had created a sense of familiarity and built up the children's confidence to follow us on the trip. The bed in *Bedtime Story* eventually floated away on a Sea of Dreams to a chorus of singing toothbrushes. We have always avoided fairy tales, nursery rhymes and the traditional kings, queens, princes and princesses which often feature in theatre for young audiences believing that the best launch pad for the imagination of the children lies in day-to-day reality.

We discovered early on that the average audience of under fives was ignorant of the convention of the fourth wall in theatre. If they were interested in our performance, they wanted to get up, talk to the characters, help them solve their problems, touch their costumes, hand them their props. We needed to open our work up to the audiences by allowing them to talk to the characters and have a say in the development of the story. It was particularly important for characters in a performance to ask the audience open questions which invited a range of responses and which would open the way to improvisation that would advance the story. Taking these factors into account, we found we could grip an audience of under fives for up to an hour.

Throughout the 1980s we created at least one new production for under fives each year, and complemented these with other productions for 5 to 9 and 7 to 11 year olds. Our shows for older children also employed a wide range of theatrical methods which included a strong visual dimension and live music, although these performances used more sophisticated verbal language, complex narratives and characterisation.

Oily Cart and children with learning disabilities

In 1988, the deputy head of a school for young people with severe learning disabilities asked us if he could book one of our shows for the under fives. I had been involved in a production for special schools during my time with the Glasgow Citizens' Theatre for Youth Company and asked if we could work instead with the school to develop a piece more age appropriate to his students, who ranged in age from 3 to 18. After playing with the students and talking to the staff for a week, we discovered that the school contained an enormous range of abilities. Some older students were articulate, mobile and could look forward to an independent life as adults. Others were young people with a complex variety of sensory and intellectual disabilities who needed assistance with the most everyday of activities. There were, of course, a great number of young people somewhere on the spectrum who fell between these two extremes. No one form of theatre was going to satisfy all the audience requirements in the school. We realised we had encountered our second 'impossible' audience.

During the brief period of research and workshops in the west London school, we made two further discoveries that have informed our work for this sector ever since. Firstly, staff were clear that if we were really to connect with the young people in the school we should rethink our ideas about the duration and location of the performance. The deputy head, for example, explained that the performers should spend a good deal longer with the young people than the usual 45 minutes to an hour-long show. Considerably more time was needed to give the young people the chance to get to know us and us, them.

In consequence our first show for special schools, *Box of Socks* (1988), took place over a whole school day. A trio of aliens from outer space crashed their spaceship into the morning assembly and spent the rest of the day wandering all over the school, mystified about life on earth. This turned out to be an empowering event for the students, who had to elucidate aspects of human behaviour from eating to writing to the extra-planetary visitors. It was especially empowering for the group from the senior department who took an alien shopping for party ingredients and spent their time persuading the creature not to demand cake in the butchers and meat in the travel agents.

Our second discovery was the importance of working with the kinaesthetic sense, the sense involved with the detection of movement of the body; for example its perception of the position and movement in space. In that first school much use was made of a technique called 'hammocking', where two members of staff would swing and bounce a young person in an old navy hammock. The process gave a great deal of pleasure to the young people, especially those with impaired vision or hearing for whom some of the main sensory pathways which connect performer and audience were blocked.

When we created *Box of Socks*, theatrical work for people with severe learning disabilities was also being pioneered by other companies, notably Interplay who are based in Leeds, and Theatre Centre in London. Nevertheless, there was very little other provision for these audiences despite a great demand from special schools. Although other TiE companies at that time, and other theatre artists in the decades since, have made occasional productions for such audiences, there remains a dearth of long-term programming for young people with severe learning disabilities. So from 1988 to the present day Oily Cart has toured at least one production for these audiences each year.

Our work for special schools has grown increasingly specialised over the years. From 1988 to 1996 our programmes, often taking place over two days in each school visited, would try to provide something for everyone in the school. We offered a range of modules pitched at different ability levels, and opened and closed moments when the whole school would be brought together. Each module might be considered a performance-based workshop in which the performers interacted in character with the participants to create a piece of theatre or an artwork that would then be used in a performance for the whole school.

Certain modules on offer would be specifically for older students who were verbal, mobile and looking forward to an independent adult life. Others would be devised for young people with little or no verbal language, considerable mobility problems and complex physical and intellectual impairment who needed assistance with most basic functions. We usually offered six modules in a programme, which could encompass the variety of abilities and ages in the school. Very often the same student would turn up as a participant on two or more modules. For example, a student would take part in one module because they were over 16 and in another because they were non-verbal and would benefit from a purely multi-sensory approach.

For example, for *Georgie Goes To Hollywood* (1994) we had created the beginning and end footage of an adventure video in the rehearsal period. Over the course of our two days in the schools we shot the other scenes for the film during the different modules. The more articulate and mobile students had speaking roles in scenes with a more or less complex narrative. But there was also a sequence called 'On Butterfly Island' that involved the young people who would now be labelled as having Profound and Multiple Learning Disabilities (PMLD).

The sequence was videoed and incorporated into the final presentation but the creative process was also enjoyed by the participants in the moment, as a series of events which delighted each of the senses in turn. It could be enjoyed as a multi-sensory delight without any further significance, or as part of a complex creation made by the whole school and the Oily Cart team, or as both. At the end of the two days the whole school would dress up for the world premiere of the film they had created.

Work for children with profound and multiple learning disabilities

In 1996 we created our first piece, *Tickled Pink*, specifically for young people with PMLD. We had come to realise that the young people with the most profound and complex disabilities not only showed some of the most astonishing reactions to our work, they also had the least alternative cultural provision. Since this realisation, all our work in special schools has been more tightly focused and nowadays we concentrate on young people labelled as having PMLD or an Autistic Spectrum Disorder (ASD).

Labels like PMLD and ASD are hopelessly reductive attempts to sum up an extraordinary range of people in an audience with a wide range of interests and abilities. For our audiences with such complex learning disabilities, Oily Cart's aim is ultimately the same as the one we have for our audiences under 5: in each production we aim to create theatre which is relevant to their view of the world and uses the languages they use. We must find themes and create characters that audience members will be interested in, and we must make theatre that can engage young people with a wide range of abilities. We know that this kind of theatre has to be multi-sensory, addressing the senses of touch, taste and smell as well as sight and sound. Our performances may involve aromatherapy, hand and foot massage, fans, foam and bubbles, in addition to characters who can be identified by the texture of their costumes, the iconic props they carry or the scented wristbands they wear.

In recent years we have focused our work to incorporate the kinaesthetic sense. As I wrote earlier, hammocking was used in many of our early productions for young people with learning disabilities, despite being hard on the backs of the performers. In 1999 we were grateful to find an alternative way of engaging the kinaesthetic sense by working in hydrotherapy pools. Our first production in such a setting was called *Big Splash*. In the pools many participants enjoy a wider range of movement than they are used to. They are freed, for the moment, from the constraints of the wheelchairs, braces and splints in which many of them have to spend their lives. The relationship between performer and participant is particularly good in the water. The two are, for the most part, on the same level, face to face. We aim for this kind of relative positioning in all our productions, and have worked continuously to avoid towering over wheelchairs or small children since our productions began.

Whilst working on the development of the hydro pool shows, ex-special school head, Eddie Anderson, encouraged us to investigate the use of trampolines. We made our first trampoline-based show, *Boing*, in 2002 and found that, as with the shows in water, the trampoline alleviated the effects of gravity and gave many of the participants a much wider range of movement than usual. Our trampoline productions also saw an increase in the involvement of people on the autistic spectrum. The schools told us that many of them were fascinated by trampolines and other g-force inducing activities. This may relate to the hypothesis that the kinaesthetic sense is underdeveloped in some people with ASD so they derive particular pleasure from activities that stimulate this part of the sensorium.

Lately we have explored the kinaesthetic sense via various forms of moving seating, placing our audiences in anything from rocking chairs, to garden swing seats. In *Something in the Air* (2009), the audience of six young people with six companions is flown up in to the air in specially designed seating, and as they swing, bounce and spin, they mirror the aerialists who fly above, beside and below them. As well as being multi-sensory, we also know that our theatre for young people with complex learning disabilities has to be highly interactive. We need to be able to continually adapt what we are doing to meet the requirements of a specific spectator. For example, in *Something in the Air* one young person will want to be winched up high, while another will prefer to stay low; one participant will want to bounce energetically while another prefers to sway gently. As we work in a very close-up way, we are able to scrutinise the reactions of the young people and their adult companions and continually adjust what we are doing to suit individual requirements.

We always try to remember that because many of our audience members have communication impairments, it is very difficult for us to know what they might be thinking. Therefore, we listen very carefully to whatever language they are using, both in our preparation for a production and during any particular performance. This was true for the productions we made for people with severe learning disabilities that were suitable for the whole school, but considerably more so when we started to concentrate on young people with ASD or PMLD.

In conventional theatre, the audience's role is to sit and watch, but in an Oily Cart show it is the performers who must watch the audience with greatest intention. They must observe the reactions not only of the young people who are the primary participants in a performance, but also of the adult companions, such as teachers or family members, that are present. Performers must be prepared to change not only the tone but also the content of their performance to suit the requirements of the individuals with whom they are working. The Oily Cart performer always has the option of returning to an approach that was effective earlier in the performance if a participant wants nothing to do with a more recently introduced stimulus.

In any audience of young people with severe learning disabilities we make the assumption that at least one of them, unable to communicate verbally, is thinking, 'I wish these clowns would bugger off so I could get back to listening to Radio Four.' Perhaps that's not always true, but it's a useful control. It means we have to create the very best work we can not only with regards to the multi-sensory and its interactive aspects, but also in terms of story and character. This means that our productions for those with PMLD and ASD must have narrative and characterisation that we, as artists, find both intellectually and emotionally engaging and, most definitely, not patronising. We must create a structure which is viable when experienced as a sequence of sensory events but which also works for those who can follow the development of characters and a narrative over the course of a performance.

In our production, *Blue*, which ran from 2006 to 2008, audience members were told a week or more before they were to attend the actual performance that they were going to visit a group of people waiting for a train. Each of these characters would have only one piece of luggage, and this contained the one thing they could not bear to part with. We asked our young audience members to think about what they could not leave behind if they had to go away from home, perhaps never to return. This request could be interpreted as asking them to choose their favourite toy. On the other hand, throughout the world there are innumerable examples of people forced to flee their homes with nothing more than what they can carry. So the production led some in our audiences to consider the situation of economic and political migrants and compare it with their own.

In all of our theatre for those with complex learning disabilities we make a 'social story', which helps our audience engage with the production. We came across the concept of a 'social story' in special schools where it is often used to help young people on the autistic spectrum, who commonly have difficulties with social interaction, new experiences and changes to their daily routine. Using graphics, the customary behaviours involved, for example, in eating in public or visiting a grandparent are explained in detail which helps the young person prepare for and deal with these events.

Theatre, we realised, involves particularly complex social interactions and we now use 'social stories' to introduce the characters in a show, the setting where it will take place and the seats the audience will be using. The stories also suggest ways the participants can prepare for the performance experience, for example by making something that will be used in the show.

Another particularly important feature of the social story as far as people on the autism spectrum are concerned is that it suggests how young people with ASD might respond to the characters. For example: 'It's OK to laugh' and 'You can say 'OK' if you would like to sit in one of the moving seats' or 'No' if you'd rather not.'

For many on the spectrum the world is potentially a very confusing place, where difficulties in processing sensory data can lead to disorientation and panic. To instill a sense of order many schools use strict schedules so students find it relatively easy to locate themselves within a task or the school day. One huge advantage of theatre for people on the spectrum is that involving them in an experience that is distilled, ordered and predictable reduces the chance of sensory overload. Armed with a social story and a timeline, a graphic illustration of the sequence of events in a show, participants can see where they are up to in a performance and anticipate the ending. I believe this predictability and sense of order are the factors which make Oily Cart's ASD work so engaging for the audiences on the spectrum.

While demystifying the theatre process is a significant part of the Oily Cart strategy, especially when it comes to productions for people with ASD, paradoxically, we sometimes adopt a completely different approach. As part of our preparations for the special schools who visited performances of our show for people with ASD and PMLD, *Blue*, for two weeks we embedded a character from the show in two of the schools. One Monday morning the students turned up at school to find that a shack had been built in their playground. One of the show's Blues singers lived in this shack for a week, cooking, washing, hanging the laundry on the line, sleeping and singing the Blues. To build up their curiosity, these characters would at first have nothing to do with the children but by the end of the week, when they accompanied their Blues character to the performance, everyone was confident and ready to meet the other characters. One of the school parties was from a school for people with ASD, and this group in particular grew significantly in their confidence and desire to communicate over the course of the five days. However, it is interesting that actors in these roles never revealed their true identity. Both the mystifying and the demystifying approaches appear to have value in terms of engaging our audiences and we would be loath to abandon either.

Our social stories are available as DVDs, as photo-illustrated stories which can be downloaded from our website and as hard copies posted in advance to schools. In addition, wherever possible, staff briefing sessions form part of an Oily Cart visit to a school. These sessions and our social stories also suggest ways that staff and parents can follow up the immense stimulus of a theatre experience and contain ideas for practical activities back in the home or classroom. At best our theatre begins long before the participants encounter a live actor, and continues to motivate activity long after the performance has finished.

We take care that our annual programme of work includes shows that visit schools and shows where schools visit the theatres. Sometimes schools prefer us to visit them, where all facilities are to hand and there is less risk of stress for young people and staff. However, though organising a visit to a theatre can be hard work, the benefits of a trip out into the wider world are innumerable. Many special schools tend to be socially isolated and inward looking. I believe it's highly desirable for their students to experience more of life outside the home and school, and for society as a whole to have more frequent encounters with this often invisible community.

Theatre for babies and infants

It took us rather a long time to realise that the multi-sensory, close-up, highly interactive form of theatre we had devised for young people with complex disabilities might be relevant to other audiences. It was not until 2001 that we began to create theatre for children aged 6 months to 2 years old, as part of our production *Jumpin' Beans*. As with young people with complex learning disabilities, babies and toddlers are another audience often thought of as impossible. After all, they are primarily pre-verbal, know little and care less about theatrical conventions and are often as interested in smelling and tasting new phenomena, including performers, as they are in looking at or listening to them.

In many other ways these two audiences could not be more different, and I am still astounded by the intense focus and speed of response of a neurotypical audience of babies and toddlers. For example, although our hydrotherapy pool production *Pool Piece* (2008) was devised for audiences of young people with PMLD and ASD, on one occasion, as an experiment, we performed to a group of mothers and babies. In this performance there were several moments where we would bring the action to a halt by sounding a very large gong that stood at the water's edge.

When the audience in the water consisted of young people who had PMLD, it would almost always take several seconds for the participants to turn to and acknowledge the source of the sound. However when the neurotypical 2 year olds heard the gong, all heads turned towards it as one, and all eyes focused on it in a split second. It was just one short moment which confirmed to me that, for a great variety of reasons, young people with PMLD or ASD can take a considerable time processing the data conveyed to them by their senses. By contrast, young neurotypical audiences have reaction times, which seem to me almost shockingly fast.

Making theatre, not therapy

I am frequently asked about the underlying justification for what we do in an Oily Cart performance, perhaps on the assumption that an educational or even therapeutic aim underpins our work. At its core, Oily Cart tries to make theatre, not therapy. It aims to give its audiences an opportunity to participate in richly layered multi-sensory work that leads in turn to additional benefits. For me the best moments occur in our performances for people with complex learning disabilities when a young person reacts in a way which surprises, even astonishes, the parents or carers who see them every day. We create complex, highly stimulating situations, and our young audiences often react in quite unanticipated ways. Adult companions can see which particular event or method caused a reaction and which can often be easily reproduced at home or in school.

But it is not just about techniques: it is also about attitudes. We put as much imagination, playfulness and attention to detail into our work as we can. Not infrequently, audience members respond in ways that challenge the labels, syndromes, and the behaviours which are hung on them. This permits them to be seen in a new light by the people who live and work with them every day. Attitudes shift, and it is my hope that the spirit, as well as the detail, of the Oily Cart's approach will become part of these people's day-to-day routine and influence their behaviour long after we have packed up our van and are on the road to our next gig.

Clearly our chosen audiences are not so impossible after all, and it is my hope that more practitioners will continue and extend our work for these young people. Better yet, I would like to see many more theatre artists seek out other sections of the community neglected by the theatre – those affected by dementia, for example – and set about making work that satisfies their particular requirements.

Oily Cart: all sorts of theatre for all sorts of kids edited by Mark Brown, giving a fuller account of thirty years of The Company, is published by Trentham Books in 2012.

10

'All this and more': learning through participation in Theatre in Education

Geoffrey Readman

Introduction

'All this and more' is a phrase which articulates the particular and unique contribution that participation in educational drama and theatre can bring to a child's education. It was coined during a two-year international research study which investigated the impact of drama and theatre in developing the Lisbon key competences in education (Cziboly, 2010). A key finding was that,

> To reach children, we need a tool that will deeply interest and engage them. We should teach them through the art form of theatre and drama, and through the dramatic role-play and stories in which they become actively engaged in exploratory investigation of moral, social or curriculum contents and what it means to be human in a contemporary world. In this way they become enabled and empowered – active and thinking citizens. (Cziboly, 2010:13)

The study concludes that there are eight competences in total that are essential in terms of their potential contribution in developing the skills, knowledge and attitude development of individuals living in a knowledge-based society. Five competences are the focus of the drama and theatre research: 'communications in the mother tongue', 'learning to learn', 'interpersonal and social competence', 'entrepreneurship' and 'cultural expression'. 'All this and more' was designated an additional sixth competence, as researchers across twelve countries were in agreement that educational drama and theatre offer something unique to growth and development, a quality which they perceived to be fundamentally concerned with 'what it is to be human' (Cziboly, 2010:19).

In a parallel development, the English school curriculum has included a strong emphasis on matters of 'citizenship', which was introduced as a compulsory subject in secondary schools in 2002. In this chapter, I suggest that if children are to begin to understand concepts such as community and family, each deemed by politicians and sections of the media to be remedies for what British Prime Minister David Cameron has repeatedly called a 'broken society', it is important to provide curriculum opportunities to engage with the tensions, benefits, conflicts and contradictions of these complex concepts. I argue that participating in Theatre-in-Education (TiE) offers young people an experience in which critical reflection and emotional engagement facilitate unique learning possibilities in ways that address these issues. Participation may not be an essential component of TiE, but when used as an aesthetic enhancement of educational intentions it can facilitate learning which goes beyond the communication of moral messages about social behaviour.

The practices of TiE

TiE continues as an innovative hybrid of theatre and education when devised for a particular age group in pursuit of both aesthetic and learning objectives. It is marked by the participation of children who are often invited to adopt fictional roles within a performance which is, in the best practice, contextualised within a programme of age-specific learning activities. Clearly, there are ethical considerations at stake in making theatre in this context, particularly when children are invited to collaborate in a process in which the performers have expertise in presentation, facilitation and, crucially, relevant pedagogy (Rifkin, 2010).

The birth, development and decline of British TiE in the second half of the twentieth century have been well documented (Reddington, 1983; Jackson, 1993; Wooster, 2007). The twenty-first century has brought further reductions in the number of TiE companies working in schools and, despite new initiatives in other parts of the world, such as Hong Kong, there has been a limited development in participatory theatre techniques (Prendergast and Saxton, 2009:33). TiE is now frequently cited within the broader generic fields of applied theatre (Taylor, 2003), theatre education, (Nicholson, 2011) and interventionist theatre (Jackson, 2007). Umbrella terms can help facilitate dialogue across the field but run the risk of obscuring the identity and tradition of individual theatre genres unless critiqued appropriately (Thompson, 2003:14).

The nature of the TiE practice described in this chapter is one that invites its audience to participate, question and explore. It engages children in complex problems and aims to raise further questions both through and within the theatre form. It does not seek to arrive at pre-defined solutions or achieve specific targets, but rather deals with difficult issues which are rooted in reality and for which there are no guaranteed outcomes. It achieves this objective through concrete and specific dramatic action that portrays human behaviour in sharply defined social contexts. Its processes rely upon theatre's potential to generate and accommodate diverse perspectives. As Brook articulates, 'theatre has the potential – unknown to other art forms – of replacing a single view-point by a multitude of different visions. Theatre can present a world in several dimensions at once' (1987:15). While this capacity is shared by all theatre, I suggest that TiE that is designed to encourage children's active participation offers learning experiences which are qualitatively distinctive and in which the participation is integral to the art form.

In the first book published about TiE, O'Toole claimed that participation, when relevantly conceived, has the potential to offer a holistic, comple-mentary experience, in which participation and theatre 'feed each other, growing together into a fusion of personal experience and projected identifi-cation, completely subjective but with its own sense of proportion, more complete and more thoroughly affecting than any presentation' (1976:88). He goes on to articulate that there are at least three categories of participation:

Extrinsic – where the element of participation is separated from the theatri-cality.

Peripheral – where the audience is invited to contribute in order to add to the theatricality without affecting either the structure or nature of the play or its own basic function as audience.

Integral – where the audience perspective becomes also the perspective of characters within the drama, especially when the audience members act as well as being acted upon. The structure of the dramatic conflict, the audience's relative position to it, and therefore the total experience are altered.

The element of theatre is no longer central. (1976:88)

Central to the definition of integral participation is a commitment to deepen-ing and extending children's learning. O'Toole goes on to claim that when children are engaged in such participation, it is possible to observe the com-mitment and intensity which they put into 'areas where they have freedom to respond how they will, and [to] watch their unshakable determination to resolve the hardest dilemma, as well as their imaginative command of all the factors which may be relevant' (1976:113). One of the key dimensions in achieving this quality is the interactive relationship between the children and actor-teacher. The actor-teacher needs the expertise to respond to the children's contributions, whilst remaining loyal to the theatrical parameters of their role.

The capacity to engage an audience directly whilst simultaneously encouraging them to participate within the art form has been defined as an ability to be 'actively – and interactively – responsive to and responsible for the dramatic narrative' (Hennessy, 1998:86). Both O'Toole and Hennessy, although writing about practice in different eras, describe a dynamic process through which children can 'become open-minded, empathetic and responsible' (Cziboly, 2010:13). TiE continues to offer a radical alternative for children, artists, teachers and, indeed, politicians.

The case studies
The following case studies are of two devised TiE programmes. They have been selected because of the structure of the participation and the manner in which it was realised. In both programmes, the children were confronted with violent behaviour, albeit within the safety of the art form. It is hoped that the case studies will illuminate the learning potential of theatre which, as Brook identifies, stimulates a multiplicity of visions. The two moments are quite different in structure and form. One of the examples, *Away from Home* (1982), performed in schools in Leeds by Leeds TiE, involves a class of primary school children, in role as evacuees who witness the shooting of an escaping German Prisoner of War. The other, *Crossings* (2011), performed in Birmingham schools by Big Brum TiE, involves an 11 year old boy, George, who overhears a conversation between his parents about the need to vacate their home due to economic crises.

Away From Home was devised for one class of 9 and 10 year old children. The class meet an actor-teacher who explains that they will be part of a story about an evacuee called Jean, a girl about their age, who she will portray. They are seated on a large rectangle of canvas which is used throughout the programme to create different locations in their school hall. Jean is told by her father that the declaration of war with Germany means she must be evacuated for her own safety. The class is then contracted into the role of evacuees and makes the fictional journey from Leeds to Filey.

Jean narrates the journey and continues to be the storyteller throughout the programme. There is much physical participation, as the class, as evacuees, move around different locations: the train, the railway station, the village hall, the beach, a bridge, the local school and an air raid shelter. The four actor-teachers perform and make their own sound effects, developing the narrative's atmosphere, mood and location with overhead aeroplanes, train sounds and air raid sirens.

When they first arrive in Filey, the evacuees are met in the village hall and are allocated to local families. Jean is billeted with a single elderly man called Mr Green, a member of the local Home Guard. He has strict house rules. At the weekends, Jean goes to the beach to play with the other evacuees. On one such visit they come across a prisoner of war camp, theatrically depicted by wire fastened to free-standing posts. The class also participates as audience members by watching scenes in Green's house. All of the movement, which is carefully guided and supported by the actor-teachers, corresponds with the mood and function of each of the scenes: they sit in small groups in the village hall; in two rows on the train; they stand in lines whilst being allocated to a family; and they move around the beach in response to Jean's narration.

The evacuees soon experience their first air raid, an experience created when the actor-teachers lift the rectangular canvas to construct a large shelter, which they all enter, led by Jean. They can hear the sounds of overhead bombers outside. The shelter creates a sense of isolation both within the fictional world of the village and, actually, within the real world of their school hall. Suddenly, a German prisoner of war enters; he can only speak one or two words of English, but explains that his name is Willi and shows the evacuees photographs of his family in Germany. On each occasion that I observed this programme, the class involved immediately formed a relationship with Willi that was warm and sympathetic.

During a secret expedition to the beach a second emergency occurs: the evacuees find themselves stranded on a dangerous part of the beach. Willi, whilst attempting to make his escape from the camp, discovers them and helps them to safety, across a bridge, one by one. In the midst of some frenetic confusion, Green appears with a gun. He misunderstands the situation, refuses to listen to the children's pleas about Willi being a friend and tells them to return to the village and Willi to the camp. The German refuses, turns to escape and is shot dead by Green.

Away from Home compels the children to confront a killing whilst maintaining the fictional role of evacuees. The narrative is pre-determined and reflection upon the events is left to the class teacher. In *Crossings*, however, they explore and discuss aspects of violent behaviour as themselves, taking on roles in order to demonstrate or give voice to their speculations. It has a flexible narrative structure which children can influence. *Crossings* is aimed at Key Stages 2 and 3 and begins in a classroom with a whole-class discussion, led by three actor-teachers. It is 'designed to have cross-phase and cross-curricular appeal' (Programme Handout, 2011). On the day I observed this programme, the facilitator posed some stimulating and provocative questions which prepared the children for their participation. The class was invited to give their views and opinions from the start, for example:

> Lead Facilitator: We are going to look at a moment that changed someone's life. Does anyone want to tell us about a moment when their life changed?

One boy describes the arrival of a new baby into his family. A girl talks about a holiday to Pakistan. The class is transformed from a rather disparate group of individuals into one group with a common purpose. They become visibly more focused and attentive. They understand that they are about to be given some responsibility for the circumstances in the narrative. The actor-teachers value everything the children offer with spontaneity and interest; each contribution is received with respect and without judgement.

At the appropriate moment, the facilitators instruct the children to leave the classroom for the hall, having forewarned them that they will see a scene about a boy called George who overhears something that 'will change everything for ever.' Once in the hall, the children are seated on chairs and in rows. They are invited to consider the kind of room that the set before them represents. The lead facilitator walks within the set, questioning the implications of the objects that are there: table, chairs, mirror, a chair in need of repair, school uniform and a letter. He asks for responses to the objects, breaking down the separation between the stage setting and the auditorium. He then sets the context for the first scene.

The children watch as George overhears that his parents are to be forced to leave their home and he must leave them to live with his uncle. They are invited to demonstrate their ideas of how George might respond to this news through dramatic action. Individual children portray George on the set. They demonstrate how George might leave the house. The actor-teachers have a range of exploratory strategies at their disposal. Unlike *Away from Home*, there is no formal script as such, only scenes which carry the potential for exploration which will be selected on the basis of the facilitator's reading of each class. At one point, an actor-teacher narrates: 'George picks up his new school shoes and scratches them with a fork.' On this occasion, groups were formed and asked to address the question: 'What causes a child to carry out such an action?'

Participation

Participation in these two examples is, I suggest, an integral dimension of the art form. The children's immediate and spontaneous responses contribute to the dramatic tension of the learning context and are the result of their willing complicity in the process of the performance. The participatory moments are intended to create an engagement with the material which combines the mental states of spectating and performing within the here and now of both fiction and reality. The narrative has been selected for its relevance to the age group and its potential for exploration.

The effectiveness of both examples relies on the creation of an engagement that is at once both immersive and critical. It allows the fictional world to be connected to and interpreted through personal feelings. There is no sense that either of these moments presents children with problems that can be resolved, as might be the case in more outcome-driven theatre. In an unpublished interview, Big Brum's artistic director Chris Cooper makes the point that: 'the heart of contemporary practice should be not to give them a problem that they can cure or solve.'

In *Away From Home* this problem is experienced by the whole class who are in role as evacuees. The shooting creates an emotional jolt that confronts them with moral dilemmas relating to nationalism, friendship and loyalty. Mr Green, a senior member of the Home Guard, is genuine in his desire to protect Jean and the evacuees but Willi has become a friend: he helped them across the bridge, he warned them when they were in danger and his escape is, after all, to see his family. The fact that they had met Willi (inside the shelter) and had listened to his family stories, told in an unsentimental way, is a vital component in avoiding received stereotypes about the war, and makes the real issues of the shooting more complex.

In *Crossings* the participation is concerned with the children taking responsibility for another person's social problem. The children are invited to interrogate and question what is happening in the narrative. They are actively encouraged to make connections with their own lives: 'What are the barriers that stop us talking to each other?' asked the lead facilitator in a response to a child's observation that the parents 'rarely look at each other'. Potential solutions for the problem are explicitly owned by the children, as they volunteer

111

to act out their own interpretations of George leaving the house or scratching his shoes. The following analysis, also from Big Brum's artistic director, illustrates how children's ownership of dramatic action can be received and interpreted. A girl enacts George leaving the room:

> She did it three times and every time she did it she walked through the wall. Some of the kids said 'she's doing it wrong.' But she wasn't doing it wrong; she was doing it absolutely right. What she was concentrating on was the shoes! So ... the wall was entirely irrelevant to her. She made us see the shoes in a way that no one has ever made us see the shoes. It was extraordinary to watch. If you are not attuned to the relationship between internal and external coherence then you would see such action as a problem.

Cooper's analysis valuably articulates a tension. Participatory action can be misunderstood by teachers and observers who anticipate that its primary aim is for the children to create characters and portray them in a convincing way for others to watch. These are rarely the criteria when participation is structured to offer the opportunity for children 'to be actively – and interactively – responsive to and responsible for the dramatic narrative' (Hennessy, 1998:86).

Devising and the actor-teacher

Devising has historically been an integral dimension of the TiE process and, I suggest, a feature of both case studies. The actor-teacher role and its relationship with children in performance exemplify differences between TiE and dominant theatre practices (Hennessy, 1998). The role involves taking responsibility for every aspect of the learning experience. The whole company should have a 'genuine commitment to the subject area they choose and the questions they raise if the mechanics of the programme, the structure, the words, actions and characters are to be of any value to the children' (Pammenter, 1993:56). There are no set procedures which define the process, although in TiE learning objectives are usually the priority from which content and form emerge.

Research is an important dimension of the actor-teacher's role; they need opportunities to explore at their own level, to articulate their position on the material from a personal perspective. They also require the opportunity to research relevant stages of child development, as they encounter many different school contexts during the course of a run. The capacity to respond to individual needs requires an understanding of the artistic, social and pedagogical implications of the programme structure. The actor-teacher should not lose sight of their individual responsibility for the child's eventual learning experience, which is being uniquely realised by the artistry and energy of a group of performers. The learning should be 'well planned, [have] depth, truth, usually ... its own internal logic and ... an artistic integrity that reaches and involves the child, [as well as being] challenging to both child and performer' (Pammenter, 1993:69).

Devising enables companies to select roles which fulfill particular functions in relation to the learning objectives. Multi-role playing, a common feature of devised theatre, facilitates a productive dissonance which can be harnessed as characters are developed in response to objectives. This capacity of children to engage with two contexts at the same time is of the highest significance for participation in TiE. It is a concept which Vygotsky termed 'the dual effect – the child weeps in play as a patient, but revels as a player' (1976:548).

The structure of both programmes draws upon this concept. In *Crossings* it is through the lead facilitator establishing belief in the scene when the invisible George overhears his parents' conversation. In *Away from Home* it is when the actor-teacher playing Willi, the German POW, enters the shelter since the children have already met this actor as the retired Major who allocated their host families. The learning benefits of this experience and of the impact of adults interacting with children within the same fictional contexts have been the subject of detailed analysis in the drama education field (Bolton, 1979; Bowell and Heap, 2001; Heathcote, 1984).

In *Crossings*, there is a sense that the children are involved in a process of collaborative, moment-by-moment devising with the actor-teachers. This style of work places a stronger emphasis on teaching skills, but requires the same degree of understanding and commitment to the material. The lead facilitator must be able to trust the support and understanding of the other actor-teachers if they are to create moments in which the whole group operates within the same fictional context, with the same agreed purpose and focus. The initial meeting of the actors and children is one strategy which establishes the parameters and clarity of the working relationship. The establishment of a working contract, through which actors, children and teachers can work and learn, is essential and should be given priority in the devising process.

The adoption of role must be executed with clarity, if children are to have the necessary protection to deal with potentially contentious material. The relationship between fiction and reality should be apparent. Ensuring this can be difficult when actors operate as facilitators, change character or become narrators of mood and location in rapid succession. It requires the skill of blending convincing portrayals whilst maintaining the critical awareness needed to make pedagogical decisions that will draw the children into the exploration. Williams (1993) makes the point that this expertise is needed from actor-teachers throughout the devising, rehearsal and performance stages. The actor in participatory TiE is inevitably involved in offering opportunities for the exploration of social opinion through the art form. They are artist and teacher, 'developing social, critical, and pedagogical skills to guide a process of critical enquiry' (Zarilli, 2002:244).

The final moments of *Away From Home* demonstrate some of the complexities of devising participatory TiE. The children are in the generic role of evacuees, they have not been given opportunities to build individual roles. Their investment in the narrative is, nevertheless, intense, as they have run away to the beach without permission and got themselves into difficulty, from which they have been rescued by Willi. When the shooting incident occurs, they watch the event as a whole group, often trying to intervene and dissuade Green from shooting. The actor-teacher playing Jean moves seamlessly from character, to narrator, to narrator in role, within the space of a few lines.

Willi: Nein, I'm going home (puts bag on shoulder)

Green: I'll shoot you!

Jean (as character): Please Mr Green!

Green: I'll shoot you!

(Pause. Willi turns quickly as Mr Green aims his rifle. They freeze.)

Jean (as neutral narrator): The German made a run for it and Mr Green shot him.

Jean (as character): You've killed him.

Green: There was nowt else I could do lass. What else could I have done, eh? If I'd let him go he'd have been in his bomber and back here killing folk. He'd 'ave 'ad no choice and I had no choice. That's war for you. (Pause) When you're older 'appen you'll understand. (Exit)

Jean (as narrator in character): I asked them to move me from Mr Green's after that and they did, but I still had to stay in Filey. Then the war ended and I went back to Leeds to me Dad.

Jean (as actor-teacher): And that's the end of Jean's story.

(They all come out of role.)

The actor-teacher portraying Jean is required to have the same sensitive awareness with regard to Jean's given circumstances as she is to the needs of the children participating and to the programme's learning intentions. This is not theatre which is aesthetically compromised by its pedagogical, social, curriculum and ethical intentions; it is theatre enriched because of the manner in which previous participatory sequences create a dynamic invest-ment in the narrative by the participants. A frequent challenge to TiE is that the theatre is compromised by the multiple intentions and concerns of the edu-cation. However, theatre which aims 'to educate or influence can truly do so only if it values entertainment, the artistry and craftsmanship that are asso-ciated with resonant, powerful theatre, and the aesthetic qualities that by definition will appeal to our senses' (Jackson, 2007:27).

Conclusion

'All this and more' describes the economical way in which drama and theatre can enable children to make connections, drawing together or even moving across other curriculum areas. The process of enactment in drama and theatre involves the exploration of different perspectives at the same time (Brook, 1987). It combines many human qualities and characteristics when participants are emotionally and intellectually engaged. More research is needed about the benefits and complexities of actors and children interact-ing within agreed fictional contexts in role, but the two case studies illustrate how participation in TiE can prompt children to consider complex and problematic circumstances, both within and outside their direct experience, in which human beings can find themselves. Participation in *Away from Home* and *Crossings* engaged the participants in a social exploration which used feelings, attitudes, knowledge and critical reflection. There were no easy solutions or answers to dilemmas, but the nature of the participation hope-fully supported the children in their efforts to clarify the kinds of values they themselves wish to see in a future society. The process of drama and theatre creates the possibility for children to imagine and envisage the kind of people they want to be within what they see as 'a society worth living in' (Cziboly, 2010:19).

References

Big Brum (2011) Programme handout for *Crossings* www.bigbrum.org.uk/archives/000116 January 2012

Bolton, G (1979) *Towards a Theory of Drama in Education*. Harlow: Longman

Bowell, P and Heap, B (2001) *Planning Process Drama*. London: David Fulton Publishers

Brook, P (1987) *The Shifting Point*. New York: Theatre Communications Group

Cziboly, A (ed) (2010) *The DICE has been cast. Research findings and recommendations on edu-cational theatre and drama*. www.dramanetwork.eu January 2012

Heathcote, D (1984) *Collected Writings on Education and Drama*. Edited by Liz Johnson and Cecily O'Neill. London: Hutchinson

Hennessy, J (1998) The theatre in education actor as researcher. *RIDE: Research in Drama in Education* 3(1) p85-92

Jackson, A (ed) (1993) *Learning Through Theatre: new perspectives on theatre in education.* London: Routledge

Jackson, A (2007) *Theatre, Education and the Making of Meanings.* Manchester: Manchester University Press

Nicholson, H (2011) *Theatre Education and Performance.* Basingstoke: Palgrave Macmillan

O'Toole, J (1976) *Theatre in Education: new objectives for theatre, new techniques in education.* London: Hodder and Stoughton

Pammenter, D (1993) Devising for TIE. In A Jackson (ed) *Learning through Theatre: new perspectives on theatre in education.* London: Routledge

Prendergast, M and Saxton, J (2009) *Applied Theatre: international case studies and challenges for practice.* Bristol: Intellect

Reddington, C (1983) *Can Theatre Teach? An Historical and Evaluative Analysis of Theatre in Education.* Oxford: Pergamon Press

Rifkin, F (2010) *The Ethics of Participatory Theatre in Higher Education. A framework for learning and teaching.* http://www.heacademy.ac.uk/resources/detail/subjects/palatine/ethics-of-participa tory-theatre January 2012

Taylor, P (2003) *Applied Theatre: creating transformative encounters in the community.* Portsmouth, NH: Heinemann

Thompson, J (2003) *Applied Theatre: bewilderment and beyond.* Oxford: Peter Lang

Vygotsky, L (1976) Play and Its Role in the Mental Development of the Child. In J S Bruner, A Jolly and K Sylva (eds) *Play: its role in development and evolution.* Harmondsworth: Penguin Books

Williams, C (1993) The Theatre in Education Actor. In A Jackson (ed) *Learning through Theatre: new perspectives on theatre in education.* London: Routledge

Wooster, R (2007) *Contemporary Theatre in Education.* Bristol: Intellect

Zarilli, P B (ed) (2002) *Acting (Re) Considered* (2nd ed.). London: Routledge

11

Being there: an examination of how children respond and interact to an immersive theatre environment

David Broster

Introduction

This chapter considers how children respond and interact with an immersive theatre experience and presents findings obtained from primary research undertaken with 9-11 year olds by the Magic Attic Theatre Company based in the University of Worcester Drama Department. Immersive theatre is itself difficult to define and there is a spectrum of work operating under this umbrella. Vanhoutte and Wynants trace its origins back to early avant-garde experiments and identify its performing arts roots in Artaud's total theatre and Schechner's environmental theatre. They offer a definition of immersive theatre as 'the sensory experience/perception of being submerged (being present) in an electronically mediated environment' (2010:47).

Although the emphasis here is within a specifically digital culture, the centrality of the audience being submerged within an environment is a key principle for such work. Trueman develops this further, observing that it places an audience 'in situations that [they] are unlikely to encounter in everyday life' (2010:online) in order to give them an emotional experience of the story that goes beyond the hearing and seeing of it.

Responses to immersive theatre have typically been varied. Theatre critic Michael Coveney notes that, 'not long ago, the audience in a theatre was there to watch a play. Nowadays, the audience is the play, or at least the protagonist in a production that is animated by the paying customer' (Coveney, 2010) and produces a predominantly negative review of You Me Bum Bum Train's performance of the same name at the Barbican Centre in July 2010. He uses terms and phrases such as 'bullying', 'coerciveness' and 'the illusion of 'empowerment' to convey his distrust of the techniques and conventions of the form. He does concede however that what he found abhorrent about this apparently extreme immersive theatre experience were possibly the very things that others found engaging.

The roots of audience participation

In the UK a re-assessment of the position of the audience and its relationship to the performance has been one of the characteristics in the development of TYA. This has been particularly developed within the Theatre in Education (TiE) movement. From its beginnings in 1964 at the Coventry Belgrade theatre, TiE developed into a hybrid form, drawing equally from the theories and practices relating to theatre and education. The synthesis of educational thinking, child development and theatre practice ultimately resulted in a TiE participatory aesthetic that located audience participation as an integral part of both process and product. This challenged accepted conventions and role divisions within both theatre and education, as Geoff Gillham articulates:

> The words 'theatre' and 'drama' normally bring to mind a composite image comprising four features: (1) actors (2) performing (3) a play (4) for us, the audience. Similarly, 'education' normally brings to mind an image of (1) a teacher (2) imparting (3) knowledge (4) to students (5) who learn it and show they have learned it by answering questions orally or in writing. (2000:65-72)

The first phase of TiE activity, particularly from the 1970s up to the mid 1980s, resulted in a methodology that began to challenge and ultimately reject traditional theatre practices as the emphasis shifted away from touring plays towards producing devised programmes. Such programmes would be typically a half or full day and would be aimed at a single class of about thirty children, an opportunity made possible because of the funding arrangements with the Arts Council of Great Britain and Local Education Authorities at the time.

The constituent parts of a TiE programme comprised dramatic elements such as character as storyteller and actors performing dramatic scenes or re-enactments, which would be punctuated by active audience participation either with the class in-role or as themselves discussing issues and events related to the programme's content. The programme would have been co-ordinated by a facilitator or actor/teacher who mediated between actor-in-role and audience to guide the programme's tasks and interactions, not dissimilar to Boal's Joker role in Forum Theatre.

The fundamental aim of the TiE programme was to present an inclusive opportunity for young audiences to actively engage with issues 'to promote learning through personal and shared experience' (Seaman, 1987:50-1). It had at its centre the conviction that theatre and drama held the key to unlock children's learning potential and that the child had something valuable to add to the process. At its heart was the desire to create a methodology that would enable focused, inclusive, dialectical exploration, stimulated by the company and developed by the young audience both in and/or out of role; at the time something that stood apart from the aforementioned traditional expectations of both theatre and education.

Anthony Hadden, artistic director of Theatre Blah Blah Blah, summarises this participatory drama as being 'a true meeting point between the worlds of education and the arts, worlds which should never have been separated in the first place' (Bennett, 2005:170). However, whilst the educational value of such practice might be evident, what could often be missing from such TiE experiences was, ironically, theatricality. Lowell Swortzell expresses a fear that 'the direction away from TiE's theatrical roots in Artaud, Brecht and Piscator may indeed be difficult to halt' (2001:246). Nicholson also refers to this and suggests that 'acting was far less important than debating and the illusion of theatre was thought to be a hindrance to young people's engagement with the ideas and 'real' situations set up in many TiE programmes' (2009:25).

The concern expressed here is that the very elements that make theatre powerful were being diluted or even lost and replaced by functional illustrations. There is however a significant value of participatory TiE beyond its contributions to education, and part of its legacy is that while pushing the boundaries of what constitutes acceptable material for young audiences it simultaneously raised the expectations of how theatre and young people connect. Together with the aforementioned theories and theatre practices, this provided the platform for the development of the Magic Attic Theatre and the case study presented here.

Magic Attic Theatre was established in June 2005 to produce work for the University of Worcester's annual Worcester Children's Storytelling Festival and involves staff, undergraduate and postgraduate students from the university's drama department. The company's research brief is to examine young audiences' responses to the theatre experience with particular attention to the interrelationship of audience, performer and space. The guiding hypothesis is that the synthesis of experiential, active engagement and rational analysis leads to deeper personal understanding. The company therefore seeks to involve the audience as an integrated part of the experience and produces work within specifically constructed environments.

The company draws upon and develops conventions, aesthetics and ideological positioning favoured by a number of first phase participatory TiE companies, along with ideas and practices related to immersive theatre. For example, active audience participation is a foundation stone of Magic Attic's work but rather than coordinating this via a facilitator or actor/teacher who remains outside of the fictional world, the function is embedded within the fictional world of the story.

Much evidence from studies of child development supports the idea that children learn through doing. Vygotsky saw the affective drive behind active play as the 'imaginary, illusory realization of unrealized desires' (Smith, 2010: 31-6). We can consider this the power of being exposed to something in and through play which has not been experienced in reality. This resonates with Trueman's notion of immersive theatre cited earlier. Since play involves doing, Magic Attic's work provides opportunities to experience as well as observe.

The performance focus is on the shared experience between audience and character (performer in-role) within a fictional environment; it offers varying levels of physical, emotional and intellectual involvement. This begins upon arrival as the audience is allocated a collective identity that provides them with a role within the fictional world. Such conventions exist across immersive theatre practices and the significance of the roles range from simple identity within the fictional world to more consequential and integrated participation where the audience member has varying amounts of autonomy to influence the narrative and action. In the case of Magic Attic's work it is about identity; a game offering the audience a position in the theatre performance that they do not actually encounter in real life.

An example of this comes from the 2005 production *Granny Twiddle's Emporium of Wonderful Things* which was aimed at 5 to 7 year olds. The company designed the production to be performed within and around a drama studio at the University of Worcester. The physical performance spaces were comprised of a 2m x 5m foyer area which led into an 8m x 14m studio which had an additional 3m opened up at one end to enable rear projection. The foyer space was decorated to create the interior of Granny's house while the main studio space became the attic, complete with beams to enclose the audience and performer and skylight for the rear projection of moving images throughout the performance. A painted patchwork carpet marked the young audience's seating area, while adult visitors could sit on strategically placed crates. The performance was then able to adopt an orbital style of presentation with the children at the centre of the action. The general attic lighting was dim and focused to give the effect of a single light bulb, but scenes were specifically lit.

In the production the story's action starts outside the studio by the 'front door' when the audience informally meet two of the other characters who will share the experience with them. The stage directions read:

> The audience arrives. On the door outside of the central performance environment is a hand painted sign on a broken piece of wood. It reads: 'Garage Sale'. Two characters, Dribble and Smudge are playing outside, acknowledging and engaging with at least some of the audience. From inside the house a radio is playing music and barely discernible voices can be heard. Laura, aka. Worm, comes out and sees the audience. She rushes back inside.

The diegetic sound bleeding through from inside the house creates a sense of a world beyond, and although only fragments of dialogue may be heard the mood of the moment is conveyed. The children's attention, particularly those nearer the front of the line, was often focused on trying to guess what lay behind the closed doors, whilst those further back tended to be more intent on the antics of the two other characters, Dribble and Smudge, who presented a visual and verbal introduction to the world beyond. The sudden entrance, disappearance and reappearance of Worm, a character the children had yet to formally meet and who, as a performer, stage-managed the event, created the dramatic moment and connection between the two, as yet, separate realities. Worm's opening dialogue is not delivered to the audience but rather to her granny and great aunt Agatha from the half open door:

> Worm: (vo) Granny? Aunt Agatha? They're here.
>
> (No reply.)
>
> (Radio is turned off.)
>
> Granny? Aunt Agatha?
>
> (Still no reply.)
>
> I'll let them in then shall I?

The audience has now been acknowledged, engaged by the drama but not yet allowed into the main performance space; nor have they been given any role other than that of audience. However, they are already aware, either directly or by inference, of the five characters central to the story: Granny Twiddle and Aunt Agatha, by name but not by sight, and Dribble, Smudge and Worm by sight but not by name. They are also made aware of the impending garage sale by the sign and that they are expected by Worm's frantic dialogue with her as yet unseen relatives. It is not until Worm appears and greets them formally that the events are contextualised and reinforced and their role is explained directly to them:

> Worm: Hiya. Wow ... I wasn't expecting quite so many of you.
>
> > Aunt Agatha said to bring a *few* friends to help ... didn't realise I'd asked so many! Still, I'm sure she won't mind ... we'll have it cleared in no time. I hope you're up for it ... the attic's full of stuff ... should make a bit of money. Oh be careful when you come through the house ... she's very house proud.

Apart from introducing character and location this places the audience at the centre of the story by confirming that they have been specifically invited, have a role to play and are in some way connected to the reality of the drama. This resonates with Boal's concept of metaxis, creating 'a state of belonging completely and simultaneously to two different autonomous worlds' (Boal, 1995:43). The audience is in the position of outside observers but are equally inside and part of the story's reality. In this case their ascribed role is passive but the potential for active involvement has been established, something that members of the young audience can later choose to embrace with varying degrees of commitment.

The second focus for Magic Attic's work extends to the performance environment itself, which creates an enclosed world within which the action emerges. It is designed to give the audience a sense of actually being there by putting them at the heart of the experience, sharing the same on-stage space as the performers, similar to Vanhoutte and Wynants' notion of 'immersion' (2010: 47). In *Granny Twiddle's Emporium of Wonderful Things* the audience was led through Granny's house and into the attic where the main performance happens.

In the 2006 production of *Bombs and Bicycles* this feature was developed further to include a number of adjoining environments. Designer Stuart Currie built these so the audience could experience different elements of the story and promenade down streets, through passageways and into the air raid shelter. The main performance space was the aforementioned studio which had been designed as a partially bombed out house where the audience were seated on sandbags in and around the set. Adjoining this space was a 1m x 10m corridor dressed with sandbags piled 2m high, which led into a 3m x 4m space where there was a large Anderson Shelter lit by a single flickering light bulb.

The production used a range of storytelling techniques including video projection onto and across the set and featured wartime songs, music and active audience involvement. Each of these environments was designed to be stimulating and immersive but, importantly, safe. Immersive theatre 'cannot make us fear for our lives; any production that stubbornly refuses to accept this is bound to fail' (Trueman, 2010:online). The aim behind the techniques adopted by the Magic Attic is to engender a sense of belonging, not fear.

The third focus for the Magic Attic's work is the material itself. One of the characteristics of TYA in the UK that is a part of the legacy of first phase TiE has been the way it has provided engagement with difficult and complex subjects previously considered unsuitable for such audiences. *Granny Twiddle's Emporium of Wonderful Things* deals with personal loss; *Behind the Barricades*, prejudice and fear; and *Bombs and Bicycles*, death and war. These productions all make use of a range of theatrical devices and humour invariably plays a significant role in the success of the experience.

Although situations are stage-managed, audiences are trusted to respond and are responded to within the reality of the moment. Central characters are normally youthful to help the audience identify with and understand the layers of the story, and most importantly, characters are three-dimensional. They are flawed. They are confident. They are vulnerable. They are, in other words, human. The stories progress as a result of characters' choices and do not rely on magic to resolve difficult dilemmas nor do they necessarily end in resolutions, happy or otherwise.

The connection between these elements can be seen clearly in the 2006 production of *Bombs and Bicycles*, which was aimed at 9-11 year olds. This was set at the time of the Second World War and the story's narrative took the audience on a journey from the outbreak of war to VE Day. It is focused on the experience of one particular family, from the father's call-up to the arrival of the telegram signalling his death. For a proportion of the performance the audience were seated on sandbags in and around the bombed out street but a key sequence involving active audience participation was included to add to the wartime experience.

The production began with a 1940s school assembly organised by an actor in role as the deputy head of the school with the audience upstanding in role as the class. This was allowed to establish itself before being interrupted by an air raid siren. The audience was then ushered down a dimly lit passageway to the air raid shelter by actors in role as air raid wardens. In the relatively confined space the children and selected characters experienced a simulated air raid. This was carefully controlled with the build up necessarily prolonged to allow the initial excitement to calm. It was important not to rush into the explosive drama of bombs being dropped as this was not just meant to be an exciting event. The pacing was slow and deliberate, to allow for uncertainty and even a necessary sense of boredom.

In these moments of inertia it was not untypical for children to really concentrate and listen out for the drone of the planes and then to alert the others when they thought they had heard something. The bombing raid itself began at a barely audible level and very gradually the volume and intensity increased as the planes appeared to fly overhead. Initial audience responses were perhaps predictable as the reactions to being led into the unknown created a collective excitement, which is also why it was important to sustain the moments far beyond what might be expected for a dramatic representation.

After the all-clear the audience was led back to the street, now filled with smoke and badly damaged. The intention was to add an emotional and sensory dimension to their cognitive learning via the theatrical experience. From the audience feedback, this was achieved with some level of success. The production, as with others, was enthusiastically received despite including some challenging content. It was the informal and anecdotal feedback from these productions that provided the impetus for the 2008 case study, *Behind the Barricades*.

Case Study

Behind the Barricades, also aimed at 9 to 11 year olds, tells the story of a close-knit community, a gang, whose lives are changed by the arrival of an unwanted and mistrusted refugee from a nearby planet. The production template is built upon the established performance aesthetic as described in *Granny Twiddle's Emporium of Wonderful Things* and *Bombs and Bicycles*, with action taking place inside an enclosed environment. This was again designed by Stuart Currie. On each side of the performance space there was a wall formed by 2.5m high corrugated sheets. These were distressed, in varying states of repair and marked with graffiti. Between these at one end there was an equally high, dark, imposing, gated wire fence and at the other a large scrim onto which was projected images of the cosmos. The light from the projections was supplemented by a subtle general lighting wash to create the atmosphere and support the establishment of the fictional reality.

The audience members were led through a darkened foyer area adorned with graffiti into the studio. Several of the gang members security-checked them before taking them inside and instructing them to choose where to sit in different areas of the set. This presented an opportunity to informally interact with different characters and create a connection with them and the environment. It produced a bond and implicated the children in the actions to come. Once in, the gate was locked completing the enclosure and securing the audience inside. Key points of interaction with the characters occurred throughout the performance, initially with the various gang members, next with the alien who is seeking refuge and finally with the alien's pursuer, special agent Anna Konda, an authority figure who holds the audience to account unless they give up the whereabouts of her quarry.

The aim of the research was to gather formal feedback relating to how young people engage with such an immersive theatre experience in terms of the experience itself and how this affected engagement with the content. Responses were gathered both during and after the performances. The study involved approximately 150 young people from different schools around the Worcester area across five performances. Permission was obtained in advanced for the performances to be discretely filmed. Two video cameras focusing on the audience were strategically hidden on the set, with a third placed away from the space to record the performance. The cameras were synchronised so we would be able to match the performance and the audience reaction after the event, using split-screen display. This method of recording has allowed quantitative data to be collected relating to audience attention span and observation of responses to particular elements of the performance. Post-performance research involved visits to the children's schools, which took place two to three weeks after they had been to the performance.

The children's ages determined the length of the feedback sessions which, following consultation with teachers, were kept to approximately one hour and broken down to involve a variety of individual and group based tasks. There were three defined sections. Part one focused on a simple recall of the story; part two prioritised impressions and analysis of character; and part three reflected on the immersive theatre experience. Activities included written and verbal feedback and included using A4 photographs of each character for name recall; a pack of 6" x 4" photographs from the story for small groups to put in the narrative sequence as they remembered it, post-it notes to individually stick on photographs of the characters and discussions resulting from 'before' and 'after' photographs. The follow-up sessions were all recorded via video camera and/or voice recorder.

The sample largely comprised children from school years 3 and 4 (aged 7 to 9) but there was also one year 6 group who were mainly 11 years old. In general, feedback did not indicate any significant differences between the groups and there were consistencies across the age ranges, with children able to articulate what they understood from the story, their impressions of the characters and their opinions of the theatre experience.

Although it is the responses to the experience that are of particular importance here, the research also highlights other results. As might be expected there were clear individual differences in readings of the performance. For example, within a single class of 8 and 9 year olds responses ranged from 'it was about space and how big it is' and 'we are not alone in the universe' to 'it's not about the outside it's about the inside of you', 'don't believe everything you hear, make your own judgement about people' and 'there is not only you in the world, there are other people too, so don't just take care of yourself.' The data offers no apparent difference in the range of readings between boys and girls and these comments are taken from across the spectrum.

Feedback also endorsed the importance of character to the success of the story. Children evidently retained strong and in some cases very detailed impressions of each character and it was apparent that every child could identify with at least one of the characters and that each character was most liked by at least someone in the audience. Interestingly, the characters the children related to most were not necessarily the characters they liked best. This was particularly evident for the alien: all the children liked him but only twenty per cent identified with him. This indicates an ability to differentiate between personal empathy and intellectual understanding and lends support to Theory of Mind research into children's cognitive capabilities and development which indicates that the ability to understand that other people's realities may be different from their own is evident from an early age (Smith, 2010:31-36).

Discussion relating to the theatre experience shows that the emotional involvement of the audience did not appear to undermine or dominate the ability for rational analysis. In fact the experiential aspect of performance, combined with the rational analysis, may be important in arriving at a deeper personal understanding as it enables an emotional response and a further level of investment with the story. After a performance of *Bombs and Bicycles*,

I overheard one young boy say to his teacher, 'That was awesome', and when he stopped enthusing about the impact of, amongst other things, the bombs, he finished by saying that hadn't realised that war would be so scary ... and loud, and he wouldn't want there to be another one.

There was also overwhelming appreciation for the immersive theatre experience, and the children were able to articulate rationally how the performance made them feel. Of the 150 participants 90 per cent had only ever experienced a pantomime, but 80 per cent of these claimed to prefer the immersive experience with only 7 per cent unsure and 3 per cent opposed. Responses reflected an initial fear, not only of the event but also in relation to the practical issues of where to sit and there not being proper chairs. They also recorded the excitement at entering something unfamiliar and how this evolved into a strong sense of feeling part of it. One young audience member said it was like being 'actually in the play ... kind of in but not ... 'it's not like 2D, it's 3D'. This also translated into the performance where the characters 'talk to you' and 'you were actually with them trying to find things out'. It was interesting that when the children spoke of the story they tended to use the first person, further confirming their feeling of being involved in the story.

Post-production feedback and video footage indicated that audience members also moved freely between watching and being actively involved in the reality of the fiction, without confusion and without having to be directed by an outside agency.

Conclusion

Even at this early stage of research, initial findings support the ideas that underpin the company's work. For young audiences it seems that when handled sensitively the experience of being involved and especially physically involved in the action is an exciting one and a positive addition to an otherwise end-on experience. Post-production feedback evidenced a strong preference for this kind of immersive experience with audiences appreciating the feeling of 'being there'.

The synthesis of this experience with well-drawn, three-dimensional characters and a good story is powerful and memorable. The responses relating to audience identification with and understanding of character are also interesting. Their comments indicate an ability in young people, in this case 9-11 year olds, to separate self from other. Finally this research supports claims that young audiences are capable of dealing with potentially upsetting material with maturity and intelligence.

References

Bennett, S (2005) *Theatre for Children and Young People: 50 years of Professional Theatre in the UK.* London: Aurora Metro Press

Boal, A (1979) *Theatre of the Oppressed.* London: Pluto Press

Boal, A (1995) *The Rainbow of Desire: the Boal method of theatre and therapy.* London and New York: Routledge

Coveney, M (2010) Stage directions: immersive theatre. *Prospect Magazine.* August. http://www.prospectmagazine.co.uk/magazine/you-me-bum-bum-train-one-on-one-theatre/ September 2010

Gillham, G (2000) The specific value of TiE and DiE to peace building. *NATD* 17(1) p65-72

Magic Attic Theatre (2005) Granny Twiddle's Emporium of Wonderful Things. Unpublished script

Magic Attic Theatre (2006) Bombs and Bicycles. Unpublished script

Magic Attic Theatre (2008) Behind the Barricades. Unpublished script

Nicholson, H (2009) *Theatre and Education.* Basingstoke: Palgrave Macmillan

Seaman, B (1987) Values education in action: a description and justification of Humberside Theatre in Education in action. *Issues in Moral and Values Education* 37 p50-58

Smith, P K (2010) *Children and Play.* Chichester: Wiley-Blackwell

Swortzell, L (2001) Trying to Like TiE. In Jackson, A *Learning Through Theatre: new perspectives on theatre in education.* London: Routledge

Trueman, M (2010) Immersive theatre: take us to the edge, but don't throw us in. *Guardian* Theatre Blog. http://www.guardian.co.uk/stage/theatreblog/2010/apr/07/immersive-theatre-terrifying-experience. July 2010

Vanhoutte, K and Wynants, N (2010) Immersion. In S Bay-Cheng *et al* (eds) *Mapping Intermediality in Performance (Mediamatters).* Amsterdam: Amsterdam University Press

12

Starting with Shakespeare: performative writing, Shakespeare and young audiences

Jan Wozniak

> But mention Shakespeare to the class and you will feel it groan.
> Cos we know that means we gotta read the script; and then write an essay.
> I can't even describe that shit; torture's probably the best way.
> It's got nothing to do with whether I respect the play; I do.
> But if you think it's reading material well you can forget it mate.

oby T, spoken word artist aged 15, wrote and performed a rap in a development workshop held by the Royal Shakespeare Company (RSC) with the Hip Hop Shakespeare Company (HHSC) in February 2010. In it, he succinctly expressed the commonplace understanding that, for young people forced to encounter his works as a written text in a classroom, Shakespeare is difficult and boring, is 'torture'. Similar views are heard at initiatives such as the RSC's 'Stand Up for Shakespeare' and the Shakespeare Schools Festival (SSF) programme, both of which propose that experience of performed Shakespeare, whether as performers or spectators, will bring young people greater appreciation and engagement with his plays (Royal Shakespeare Company, 2008; Shakespeare Schools Festival, 2009). Toby T's 'respect [for] the play' as opposed to the works as 'reading material' would seem to support these initiatives. However, his rap continues:

> I'm in two minds.
> I think his work is definitely something to celebrate;
> To re-adapt, yes.
> But I'm not sure should it be used to educate.
> For me watching a Shakespearean play is just pleasure for pleasure's sake.

Both the RSC and the SSF emphasise the value of performance in supporting students' educational attainment and experience of Shakespeare. Thus, rather than being for pleasure, Shakespeare in performance is used in such contexts to aid understanding and analysis of the written text in an educational setting. The student is prompted for the correct response, written in an accepted academic format, as determined by adult experts. Young people's experience of Shakespeare is thus continually mediated through adults, with teachers, academics and theatre professionals telling them what they should think of Shakespeare, how they should approach Shakespeare. As David Worster puts it, 'Shakespeare remains the property of the experts, while students remain alienated, distanced by the tissue-paper layers that they cannot ordinarily perceive but somehow vaguely realize are there' (2002:368). Worster cites Walker Percy's criticism of this presentation of Shakespeare to young people as an experience akin to consumer culture, which they can never completely own. Like Worster, Percy believes that people need to have 'sovereignty over experience' (Percy, 2005:478; cited in Worster, 2002:368)

The context of the research

My research into the meanings which are made during the performance of Shakespeare for young people aims, as far as possible, to acknowledge and promote the sovereignty of young people's experience, rather than measure the success of particular methods of adaptation in making the works more accessible. There is a wealth of research on the teaching of Shakespeare, including the use of performance in teaching (Shand, 2009; Stredder, 2009). There is also a growing field of scholarship which focuses on textual adaptations and appropriations of Shakespeare for young people (Miller, 2003; Chedgzoy et al, 2007; Hateley, 2009).

However, such research accepts *a priori* that Shakespeare is of value to young people, whilst acknowledging its potential difficulty for them. It tends therefore to concentrate on the best ways in which to convey this value. Where young people are interviewed or spoken to about Shakespeare, this is generally restricted to the effect on their understanding of Shakespeare's text and the subsequent impact on grades. Whilst I do not want to necessarily challenge the notion that experience of Shakespeare is valuable, I want to examine their experience without making such assumptions and explore what value they themselves place on it.

For an early case study in my research I worked with members of Press Gang, one of the regular youth groups offered at Theatre Royal Bath, to cover the biennial Shakespeare Unplugged festival staged at the venue's egg theatre.

During the festival, in February and March 2010, Press Gang was comprised of ten young people aged between, 9 and 15. I conducted two workshops before it started, two short sessions during the festival, followed by one group interview afterwards. Press Gang is advertised as being for 'budding young writers and theatre goers' and offers the opportunity to 'get involved in every aspect of the egg's work' (Theatre Royal Bath, 2009:68). Although they had been introduced to progressive forms of approaching performance documentation through sessions with New Generation Documentors (New Generation Documentors, 2010), a journalistic approach dominated, under the guidance of a professional practicing journalist. The young people produced reviews and articles for the Theatre Royal's website on the lines of typical newspaper theatre reviews. They identified plotlines, character portrayals, assessed performances and proffered some expression of personal like or dislike.

The professional journalistic guidance clearly gives the young people useful experience but it is limited to an instrumentalist approach to writing in the pre-determined style of theatre critics. This approach examines similar areas to those that emerge from a literary approach to Shakespeare, concentrating in the final analysis on a textual basis for performance. Although not part of formal education, the young people's experience here is similar to the pre-determined formats demanded in their educational experience.

After I asked to research the festival, Kate Cross, Artistic Director at the egg invited me to work with the group as fully as possible. I hoped to interview administrators, performers and audience members. The focus on investigating, documenting and writing about performance fitted my interest in what the young audiences themselves thought about performance, while my involvement was seen by the organisation as a means to involve Press Gang more directly in the festival. This was perceived to have been lacking in previous festivals, whereas the youth groups which focused on acting and theatrical production were fully involved. One of the aims of the Theatre Royal's Education Department was to have every member of every youth group involved in some way.

The artistic directors target young people. The programme and promotional material describe it as 'Shakespeare, deconstructed and reconstructed for a 21st century audience' (Theatre Royal Bath, 2010:2). Although there was no formal link to any educational programmes, the experience was still largely framed as educational. The manager of the egg significantly identified the Shakespeare Unplugged festival as attracting a markedly different, and new, audience compared to the regular audience at the egg. Ticket sales showed that 31 per cent of tickets for Shakespeare Unplugged were purchased by new bookers at the Theatre Royal and accordingly he identified this audience as 'seeking valuable extra-curricular educational experiences' for their children, whereas the egg's regular audience sought 'family entertainment' (Baker, 2010).

This is consistent with Michael Bristol's identification of how Shakespeare functions in terms of building taste communities:

> Teachers hope that Shakespeare can be the *antidote* for the debilitating effects of the culture industry. This view is endorsed by anxious parents hoping that school bus trips to the local Shakespeare festival might save them from the seductions of rock videos. (1996:93)

Thus the manager of the egg believes that the adults who bring the young people see Shakespeare Unplugged as aesthetic education. It is adults, usually parents or teachers, who mostly determine what theatre children attend.

It is notable that the companies performing at the festival shared a Platonic idea of art as education, whereby their performances produce educative truths. Such truths were commonly expressed as opposing the dominant presentation by mass media. The performers and practitioners interviewed constantly spoke about the value which theatre in general, and Shakespeare in particular, gave to young people, particularly by its contrast to the mediatised and consumerist society which dominates their lives. This attitude manifested itself in my interviews with members of Theater Gruene Sosse, who spoke of their 'poor theatre aesthetic' and explicitly acknowledged the influence of Grotowski (Grotowski and Brook, 1968).

The approach was also evident in performance. Each show was geared towards further thought about the works of Shakespeare. For instance Theater Gruene Sosse's adaptation of *Henry V* continually asked whether it is right to watch a war throughout the performance. Similarly, the *Animated Tales of Shakespeare*, presented by en masse theatre company and aimed at the youngest audience, finished their storytelling sessions by telling the children they could soon go and experience the 'real thing'. Their performances were, it seems, merely an introduction to a valuable body of work.

No matter how entertaining the children found a performance, the adults around them expected that this would be yet another educational experience. These performances were introductions both to the works and the experiences which young people encounter in education, a challenge to understand messages transmitted to them from 400 years ago.

The research focus

I sought to expand the research on children's experience of adapted Shakespearean performance beyond measuring the success or failure of such projects in educational terms. I drew on the work of Jacques Rancière by including the voice of young people in the discussion. To the extent that I wanted to offer young people the opportunity to voice their opinions in the form which they chose, my intervention here was a political one, in line with Rancière's definition of politics as:

> the configuration of a specific space, the framing of a particular sphere of experience, of objects posited as common and as pertaining to a common decision, of subjects recognised as capable of designating these objects and putting forward arguments about them. (2009a:24)

To offer young people a means of commenting on their experience of Shakespeare in a different manner to that expected in education is to reconfigure the discursive space of Shakespeare and to recognise these young people as capable of putting forward valid arguments and opinions about Shakespeare.

My research followed Reason's ethical approach to 'involve the young audience members themselves as active researchers in an open investigation into their own perceptions and experiences of ... *live* theatre performance' (Reason, 2006a:132). I emphasised to the participants that this was not an educational exercise – I was not trying to determine correct answers. Reason's note to his workshop participants is central: 'We don't want to tell you things or analyze what you are saying in any mysterious way. We just want to find out about your experiences' (Reason, 2006a:133). Despite careful attempts to minimise the educational nature of these experiments, however, young people do seek to please, to provide what they believe the right answer.

There were some important differences from Reason's research, both in terms of the environment within which I conducted my investigations and in my ideological approach. Reason describes a generational negotiation of space in his research, where 'theatre-going is a learned activity' and young people need to 'learn to be able to concentrate on the performance' rather than what is going on around them (Reason, 2006b:240).

The performances at Shakespeare Unplugged were generally in the egg, a space which is already shared between generations. The environment differed therefore from the situation Reason describes where children are expected to conform to an already determined code of behaviour. Part of the building which also accommodates the Theatre Royal and the Studio, the egg itself was built especially for children and young people, some of whom were involved in the design consultation process so as to provide a space which met their needs. I was also interested in how young people negotiated their own modes of acceptable behaviour within their own theatre space.

An adapted form of performative writing seemed appropriate to my research. Emerging out of the notion of performative utterances, Pelias argues that the performative writing which occurs under the auspices of a number of different disciplines 'cannot be reduced into a single logic' (2005:417). However, the interest in the form of the writing as much as the content, the concentration on autobiographical content and the 'affective and emotional experience of the writer' (Freshwater, 2009:23) seemed to offer the opportunity to introduce a new mode of writing to Press Gang and allow both me and the participants to research their own experience of performance, as opposed to any inherent qualities or elements of the performance itself.

Freshwater notes that performative writing 'highlights an individual experience of spectatorship ... and provides a valuable reminder that emotional and embodied responses have a significant and legitimate role in the analysis of performance' (2009:24-5). She goes on to point out, however, that:

> this approach can open itself to accusations that it fails to situate the perfor
> mance within a broader social context, that it replaces rigorous research with
> self-indulgent soul-searching, and that it ultimately tells us more about the
> writer than about the work being commented upon. (2009:25)

Although Freshwater's reservations are valid, her decision not to situate performance in a broader social context did not affect my aim to access the experience of the young writer in whatever manner emerged. Performative writing was an experiment in providing a different means of expression concerning their experience of the young people.

Practising performative writing

I introduced the idea of performative writing to the young people in a 90 minute workshop three weeks before the festival began, and invited them to listen to some music, as an example of performance, and to write immediately about what thoughts, feelings and memories were prompted, not concerning themselves with trying to describe the performance or about their grammar. I played them various interpretations of Shakespearean text, including music from Kneehigh's *Cymbeline* and The Heavy Metal Shakespeare Company. I hoped to emphasise my interest in what they thought, felt and remembered about performance while introducing notions that Shakespeare existed in many different forms.

At the end of the session, I shared with them an example of performative writing: a version of Peggy Phelan's writing in response to Marina Abramovich's *The House with the Ocean View*. I had edited this for appropriate content but mainly to remove direct reference to the performance and accentuate the personal aspect of the writing.

Phelan originally decided to explore a new way of writing because Abramovich's work 'asks us to revise our own relation to the tasks of everyday life. In my own case, that means the task of writing about performance' (Phelan, 2004: 20). My aim was to introduce to this group of young people the possibility of revising their relationship to the task of writing about performance and to write in different ways from the conventional review. Additionally, as Shelley Manis notes, Phelan's 'written engagement with performance becomes a performance itself: a collage of summary, analysis, and evaluation' (2009:147) so I was hoping to encourage my group 'to conceptualize themselves not simply as critics outside the authority of performance itself when they write, but as engaged artists in a partnership with performance' (Manis, 2009:147).

The young people produced short pieces of writing. Whilst the enthusiasm of their response varied, all made connections to their personal experience, the music prompting them to recall family members or to relate it to stories they were in the process of writing. On hearing 'Fear No More the Heat of the Sun' from Kneehigh's *Cymbeline* Flora, 15, wrote of her feelings of regret because this was her last year with a choir with which she sang this sonnet. We discussed the opportunity to develop these thoughts, linking her feelings of grief at finishing with the choir to the melancholy strains of the sonnet, which is plainly a contemplation of passing.

The initial responses indicated to me that a kind of performative writing which enabled them to concentrate on their own experience, rather than on remembering what was happening on stage or understanding what was being said, might produce valuable insights into how young people experienced performance.

The need for Press Gang to have some involvement and presence during the festival so the requirements of the Education Department were met, combined with my desire to incorporate any ideas the young people had for involvement, led to exploration and discussion of various options at a second workshop a fortnight later. Press Gang members decided to write letters to

Shakespeare, for display at the opening event. This idea grew out of an exercise aimed to develop a notion of dialogue between the young people and Shakespeare that differed from the normative relationship where they were merely asked to listen to his words. They asked questions of me in role as Shakespeare, and I asked questions of them. I hoped to provoke a critical engagement with their own experience and its difference to that of Shakespeare.

The young people responded enthusiastically, excited by the interest shown in them and their lives. Our discussion strayed far from the topic of Shakespeare, as we began to talk about their interests – in this case in the television series *Doctor Who*. In an educational setting, such straying would need to be stopped or redirected toward the topic under consideration. But I wanted to explore the young people's experience and the meanings they gave to it and the links they made.

I followed an ethnographic interview protocol for two reasons. Firstly, I hoped that by expressing my interest and participating in these seemingly extraneous and irrelevant discussions the young people would be encouraged to be more comfortable in my presence (Crang and Cook, 2007). Secondly, my focus 'on learning the meaning that the participants hold about the problem or issue, not the meaning that the researchers bring to the research or writers express in the literature' (Creswell, 2009:5) meant I did not want to miss any potentially interesting links during my data collection stage, no matter how seemingly irrelevant (Stewart *et al*, 2006:170-1; Creswell, 2009:130-1). Crang indicates how he draws on Benjamin in his own ethnographic work, highlighting 'apparently contrasting pieces of information' demonstrate new and disruptive truths by juxtaposition (Crang and Cook, 2007:183).

The letters themselves were instructive, identifying the elements of their own lives which they wanted to communicate and the areas of Shakespeare's life that interested them. Flora's letter to Shakespeare highlighted the differences in education in Shakespeare's times and in our own, drawing attention to the centrality of Shakespeare in education and the centrality of education in her life. Olim's letter tried to describe television in a manner which recognised the completely alien nature of such a concept of communication to a seventeenth century person, thus revealing the pervasive influence of television on his life.

The letters challenged the customary position of subservience to Shakespeare, of being asked to watch, listen and hear him. Their letters not only asked questions of Shakespeare, they also described their world to him; they sought to communicate with Shakespeare rather than experience him by receiving great art works by him. By encouraging this approach to Shakespeare, I drew explicitly on the presentist approach to Shakespeare described by Grady and Hawkes, who observe, 'Of course we should read Shakespeare historically. But given that history results from a never-ending dialogue between past and present, how can we decide whose historical circumstances will have priority in that process, Shakespeare's or our own?' (2007:3).

To an extent the letters exercise suggested a desire to talk to the dead – something Grady and Hawkes consider to be unhealthy in Shakespeare studies. However, I characterise the attitude they criticise as a desire to listen to the dead. For the purposes of this exercise, I had to stress the idea of a dialogue and to prioritise the relationship of the young people to their historical circumstances in an attempt to redress the bias toward the importance of Shakespeare and his historical context. I sought to follow Grady and Hawkes in pursuing an engagement with Shakespeare that 'takes a respect for the present as the basis of a critical stance' that 'will not yearn to speak with the dead. It will aim, in the end, to talk to the living' (Grady and Hawkes, 2007:4).

Once the festival started, members of Press Gang displayed their commitment and ability to understand and interrogate their experience of performance. Not that this was produced by one or two performative writing exercises; rather, it was evidence of the young people's ability to be engaged spectators. This emerged in discussion with the young people, most notably at a performance of the Paintertainer at the opening event of the festival. The performer produced a painting on a large canvas on stage in front of his audience at the egg. The painting depicted Shakespeare wearing a large gold chain and surrounded by landmark buildings. The Paintertainer made no acknowledgment of the audience, keeping his back to them most of the time, and the music playing on the portable stereo system seemed to be more for his own benefit than that of the audience.

Other members of the audience seemed focused on other matters and mostly stopped attending to the performance. But members of Press Gang began to discuss what was being painted, picking out and interrogating details of what might be a building. They propounded theories of how the artist expected his audience to react, whether people should be talking or whether this was disrespectful. They concluded that the performance may as well have taken place in the cafe and not the main auditorium of the egg, because the attention of the audience was not wholly on the performance.

Interestingly, these young people seem to have already begun learning the codes for behaviour at performances which Reason describes. They expect silence at a performance and for the audience to concentrate on that rather than on their own experience. In their engagement with this performance and each other they were more animated than I had ever seen them. When I asked them afterwards whether they had enjoyed the performance, they were overwhelmingly enthusiastic. While watching they reflected on their experience, questioned it and possibly acknowledged a change in their perception because of the unusual nature of the performance.

Their critical stance toward their experience of performance was evident in further discussions, although I often had to work to elicit responses beyond 'cool' or 'boring'. This reflects, I think, the dominant manner in which young people do encounter and engage with cultural products. The existence of fan sites and fan fiction sites for a plethora of different cultural forms shows that some young people will spend time considering and developing their relationship to their entertainment and culture but most do not consider entertainment beyond this peremptory opinion. Prompting them to consider further might replicate a school experience and I wanted to avoid doing this. I wanted to stress that this experience was not meant to be like school, where they might be expected to understand performance and produce work relating to it. The downside of this approach was that I felt unable to demand a written response as this would have felt too much like setting homework.

So the insights, ideas and reflections which began to emerge during the performance of the Paintertainer were scarely expressed in written work, and the few written reviews produced did not deviate significantly from the dominant mode of newspaper reviews they had always followed. This was partly because I had too little time to build a trusting research relationship in which to develop and practise further ideas of performative writing. The young people saw contact with me as an opportunity to discuss and develop ideas, rather than to write individually; once at home, individual writing reverted to type and I had no chance to prompt other approaches or to encourage a reflection of their own experience instead of simply what was happening on stage.

Where access to young people is more extended, however, and work is produced during the contact time, results from an implicitly presentist approach which emphasises the centrality of the young person's experience or the dialogue between them and Shakespeare appear to produce written work which differs from the normative educational or journalistic approach. This is evident in the work of Lois Burdett, who teaches in primary schools in Stratford, Ontario. She uses the annual Shakespeare Festival and the town's links with Shakespeare to focus her whole year's work on Shakespeare. In a cross-disciplinary, cross-curricular approach, she involves all her students in studying a play for a whole year and they attend a live performance. They produce work of all sorts (writing, drawings, maps) to explore their world and their experience through Shakespeare, rather than concentrating on Shakespeare as a subject of study (Burdett, 2003).

This was also the case at a workshop at the Shakespeare Unplugged Festival, run jointly between the RSC and HHSC. Unlike the limited and rather disjointed access I had with Press Gang, these workshops ran over three consecutive days and culminated in the performance of work they had created using themes or extracts from Shakespeare. Schools referred children to the project whom they perceived to be interested in writing or performance but disengaged from their school work.

These workshops clearly succeeded in engaging the participants with writing and performance: nearly everyone performed some of their own expressive work on the performance night at the end of the week. One young person, who I observed as reluctant to join in the opening exercises on the first day was participating enthusiastically by day three in games led by Cicely Berry, though unrelated to rap. The confidence and enthusiasm that had built enabled him to discover and embrace new, different and potentially challenging experiences.

Although I celebrate the expressive work, I do not regard the less articulate responses as failing to produce interesting research findings. All responses should be considered so we can expand the number and type of voices which contribute to the discussion of performance experience. Nine year old Olim, for instance, repeatedly prefaced his verbal descriptions and written work of what he saw as brilliant by the words 'I can't get it into my head'. Olim's inability to formulate a more articulate response indicates not failure but a thoroughly engaged aesthetic and artistic experience – the 'incapacity of the imagination to grasp the monument as a totality' – which is how Rancière describes the Kantian sublime (2009b:96).

Historically, performance description and criticism has remained in the hands of a small elite of newspaper critics and theatre academics, and our knowledge of audience reactions to performances are based largely on published reviews (Postlewait, 2009:240-44). While there is limited scope to recapture the historical experience of ordinary audience members, however, we can do something about audience research now. If we reject such responses as Olim's as uninteresting or unimportant, we risk dismissing how audiences respond to live performance and potentially limit the consideration of the live event to the professionals or academics whose experience, training and function differ from the majority of the audience. If we exclude this majority, we will be unable to extend the distribution of the sensible.

Asking, and acknowledging, the views of the real audience may evoke mundane responses such as 'cool' or 'boring'. Reason acknowledges this in his research with young audiences: their reactions may confirm what we think we already know about audience experience of theatre, that it is the liveness, the potential for mistakes and so on, that are valued. To consider these supposedly mundane reactions is to accept a potentially different order of experience of performance to those which dominate the academic literature. If we let the educationally-based response dominate we are not paying attention to how young people already approach performance. I advocate acceptance and acknowledgement of all reactions to performance, whether artistically expressive or seemingly mundane. In this I follow Alan Read in wanting to speak, at least in part, for those subjects...

> ignored elsewhere for their banality, sad scale or plain unattractiveness ... not for any intrinsic political merits each might have, but rather for the way that each disrupts our expectations as to what might be worthy of attention in the first place. Along with Jacques Rancière, I am less interested in the part of those who already dominate the aesthetic airwaves by flaunting the old *avant-garde* credentials and more interested in those who until now have never entered the scene. (2008:177)

All the Press Gang participants chose their own pseudonyms.

References

Baker, L (April 2010) Interview with author

Bristol, M D (1996) *Big-time Shakespeare*. London: Routledge

Burdett, L (2003) 'All the Colours of the Wind': Shakespeare and the Primary student. In NJ Miller (ed.) *Reimagining Shakespeare for children and young adults*. New York; London: Routledge

Chedgzoy, K, Greenhalgh, S and Shaughnessy, R (2007) *Shakespeare and childhood*. Cambridge: Cambridge University Press

Crang, M and Cook, I (2007) *Doing ethnographies*. London: SAGE

Creswell, J W (2009) *Research design: qualitative, quantitative, and mixed methods approaches*. Los Angeles and London: SAGE

Freshwater, H (2009) *Theatre and Audience*. Basingstoke: Palgrave Macmillan

Grady, H and Hawkes, T (2007) Introduction: Presenting presentism. In H Grady and T Hawkes (eds) *Presentist Shakespeares*. London: Routledge

Grotowski, J and Brook, P (1968) *Towards a poor theatre*. Preface by Peter Brook. Holstebro: Odin Teatret Forlag

Hateley, E (2009) *Shakespeare in children's literature: gender and cultural capital.* London: Routledge

Manis, S (2009) Writing as performance: using performance theory to teach writing in theatre classrooms. *Theatre Topics* 19(2) p139-151

Miller, N J (2003) *Reimagining Shakespeare for children and young adults.* New York; London: Routledge

New Generation Documentors. http://www.ngds.org.uk/ January 2010

Pelias, R J (2005) Performative Writing as Scholarship: An Apology, an Argument, an Anecdote. *Cultural Studies – Critical Methodologies,* 5(4) p415-424

Phelan, P (2004) On seeing the invisible: Marina Abramovic's The House with the Ocean View. In A Heathfield, A and H Glendinning (eds) *Live: art and performance.* London: Tate Pub.

Postlewait, T (2009) *The Cambridge introduction to theatre historiography.* Cambridge: Cambridge University Press

Rancière, J (2009a) *Aesthetics and its discontents.* Cambridge: Polity Press

Rancière, J (2009b) *The Emancipated Spectator.* London: Verso

Read, A (2008) *Theatre, intimacy and engagement: the last human venue.* Basingstoke: Palgrave Macmillan

Reason, M (2006a) Young audiences and live theatre Part 1. *Studies in Theatre and Performance* 26(2) p129-144

Reason, M (2006b) Young audiences and live theatre Part 2. *Studies in Theatre and Performance* 26(3) p223-240

Royal Shakespeare Company (2008) *Stand Up for Shakespeare: A Manifesto for Shakespeare in Schools*

Shakespeare Schools Festival (2009) *Shakespeare Schools Festival Programme*

Shand, G B (2009) *Teaching Shakespeare: passing it on.* Oxford: Wiley-Blackwell

Stewart, D W, Shamdasani, P N and Rook, D W (2006) *Focus groups: theory and practice.* Thousand Oaks and London: SAGE

Stredder, J (2009) *The North Face of Shakespeare: activities for teaching the plays.* Cambridge: Cambridge University Press

Theatre Royal Bath (2009) *Theatre Royal Bath Programme* December 2009 – April 2010

Theatre Royal Bath (2010) *Shakespeare Unplugged Programme*

Worster, D (2002) Shakespeare performed: performance options and pedagogy: Macbeth. *Shakespeare Quarterly* 53(3) p278-362

13

Interviewing children after performances

Jeanne Klein

TYA artists around the world often create theatre from their speculations or implicit theories about childhood based in part on children's observable behaviours enacted during performances. In contrast, artists, such as David Holman and Tony Graham in the UK (Bennett, 2005) consult directly with young people before they dramatise and stage their stories to ensure optimal communication of their artistic intentions. As with other disciplinary rifts between theory and practice, these common artistic practices remain divorced from the theories and evidence of child audiences as published by academic investigators.

Since the 1980s, international researchers have conducted reception studies for many different reasons; for example: to discover what theatrical elements remain in long-term memories (Deldime and Pigeon, 1988:18); to determine how frequent drama and theatre experiences affect children's interpretations of productions over time in comparison to those with no drama experiences (Saldaña, 1996:67); to compare differences between expert and novice judgements of theatre (Schonmann, 2006:126-27); and to explore how children remember and respond to theatrical experiences (Reason, 2010:47-9). In such cases, investigators employ dramatic theories, such as semiotics (Deldime and Pigeon), aesthetic distance (Schonmann), and phenomenology (Reason), as methodological frameworks for analysing the evidence inductively using various tools and methods, such as questions, photographs, and drawings in individual and group interviews or behavioural workshops. As a result, we end up with an accumulated assortment of children's responses to theatre productions that keep traditional dramatic theories and beliefs about children's competences intact whilst having few consequential effects upon subsequent artistic and educational practices for future productions (Winston, 2003).

In addition to using similar dramatic theories, I have employed a more critically reasoned process that involves both the inductive and deductive separation and coordination of cognitive developmental theories and evidence (eg. Kuhn, 2011). I first review all previous child development evidence on a given topic to particularise new and yet-to-be-answered research questions and then operationalise these questions by wording more specific interview questions to ask children. Where subsequently analysed evidence contradicts a given theory or artistic belief, I attempt to revise such theoretical beliefs deductively to better explain the particular evidence. For example, presentational or Brechtian forms of theatre do not necessarily induce children to distance their emotions and think more critically about dramatised concepts by applying thematic metaphors to their own lives. Under the age of 8 or 9, children tend to regard both presentational and representational performances objectively by recounting explicit images and dialogue until they recognise the need to infer, connect and apply the causes and consequences of dramatised actions as metaphoric expressions of their lives (Klein, 1995:62-4).

The purpose of this chapter is to detail the interview questions I have used to offer researchers and artists additional strategic ideas on the art of questioning children after performances. Artists and researchers alike need to consider particular questioning methods conducive to the nature and nurturing of children's minds and emotions from their developmental perspectives. During post-performance interviews, children's aesthetic responses to theatre depend largely upon the specific questions they are asked to answer and whether they are asked to articulate their appreciations or criticisms of productions created by adult artists. Appreciation involves questions that explore whether children appreciated adults' artistic intentions to please them according to their aesthetic preferences and criterial values. In such cases, children may not express whether or not artists succeeded or failed to communicate their intended meanings for fear of hurting adults' feelings regarding all their hard work.

In contrast, questions of criticism ask children to infer artists' intentions based on the meanings they perceived and comprehended from staged actions. By asking children to interpret what artists were trying to do when expressing various metaphors and main thematic ideas, researchers can compare their speculative interpretations against artists' known intentions to determine degrees of artistic success and thereby place the public obligation and ethical responsibility of criticism on adults (Klein and Schonmann, 2009: 64-6).

From 1986 to 2003, I conducted six reception studies with 340 children aged 6 to 13. With girls making up 55 per cent of the participating group, the children were from all socioeconomic neighbourhoods in Lawrence, a predominately white city located in Kansas in the central United States. Employing methods adapted from research into the reception of television, each study focused on particular areas of cognitive and affective understanding. Specific objectives were based on the unique characteristics of each realised play. The first three studies used the plays *Don Quixote of La Mancha* (1986), *Monkey, Monkey* (1988) and *Noodle Doodle Box* (1989) to explore national curricular standards or basic comprehension of plot structures, characters' actions, and themes with one grade [year] level each to compare results against developmental findings in television studies (Klein, 1987; Klein and Fitch, 1989; 1990). The last three studies (Klein, 1993; 1995; 2003) plumbed fantasy and reality conventions, empathy constructs and computer-animated conventions among three grade [year] levels to compare developmental differences across age groups in relation to the following plays: *This Is Not a Pipe Dream* (1990), *Crying to Laugh* (1992) and *Dinosaurus* (2001). Throughout this research, questions emphasised the extent to which children rely upon visual, verbal and psychological modes of perception when interpreting meanings from respective plays in performance.

The combined results of these studies culminated in a model of aesthetic processing in theatre that coordinates and integrates multiple factors involved in perceiving, interpreting and evaluating live performances (Klein, 2005). Subsequent to this work, I have considered how four recursive stages of personal epistemology apply to performance criticism as another means of analysing child and adult spectators' critical responses to theatre (Klein, 2009). I have also explained how and why actors' mockeries of childhood in humorous entertainment deceive child and adult spectators surreptitiously, based on how children interpret humour and evaluate actors' bodies on stage and screen (Klein, 2010).

Procedures

A description of basic procedures is necessary to contextualise this work. Before the children attend the theatrical production, teachers are asked not to use study guides to assure that all responses come from performances only and not from any educational preparation. Children are bussed from their schools to attend weekday matinees of productions performed by university students in a large proscenium auditorium on campus. Participating children in each study, whose parents have signed permissions, are seated with their classmates in the centre front orchestra, with the youngest class groups in front and successively older class groups behind.

One day after attendance, fifteen minute interviews (as limited by the school district) are conducted and audio-recorded with individual children in quiet spaces at their schools. Interviewers include undergraduate and graduate students who have been trained in protocols, as well as myself. Interviewing individuals, rather than pairs or small groups, frees children from answering questions based on peer pressures (Saldaña, 1996:68). One-day delayed recall also evokes those most salient images and conceptual ideas that remain in the short-term memories of the young people.

After transcribing interviews, responses to all questions are analysed and coded by myself and two independent evaluators to assure at least 85 per cent reliability among three interpreters. Data are coded in both qualitative and quantitative ways based on respective measures. Likert-scale measures are assigned high to low numbers or zero for 'don't know'. For instance, under-standing is coded as (4) hard, (3) sort of hard, (2) sort of easy, and (1) easy.

Responses to open-ended questions are analysed repeatedly for emerging patterns of concrete to abstract categories before assigning ordinal numbers to each sub-category by (1) the presence or (0) the absence of specific vari-ables. In other words, translating qualitative ideas into quantitative variables provides descriptive frequencies of responses for respective questions. Using statistical software, frequencies, chi-squares, Pearson correlations and one-way analyses of variances (ANOVAs) are tabulated to interpret descriptive means, relationships and age and gender variations.

Rating enjoyment, understanding, and motivation

After obtaining a child's verbal assent to be interviewed and audio-recorded, the interviewer first stresses that, 'When people see plays, they have lots of different ideas and feelings about the story and the way it was done. So I'd like to know what *you* think and feel about the play you saw yesterday.' To rate general enjoyment or appreciation, we ask, 'Do you think (the same) graders in another city would like this play a lot, a little, or not at all?' Few children are willing to admit 'not at all', but asking how much their peers may have en-joyed the play lessens the social desirability factor to some extent. 6 to 8 year olds are more likely to report high enjoyment than 9 to 12 year olds, especially when attendance at theatre offers them a novel experience not provided by their parents.

To rate general comprehension, we ask, 'Was this play easy or hard to understand?' If both, then we ask, 'Was it real or sort of (easy or hard)?' followed by 'What made it (answer) to understand?' Plays intended for 6 to 8 year olds have been rated on the 'easy' end, whilst plays for 9 to 12 year olds have garnered more mixed ratings. Children tend to rate plays easier to understand when they recall more visual and especially verbal cues and when they make more psychological inferences from implicit information.

Children found plays 'hard' to understand for three main reasons. The first was where not knowing the stories, events, characters and vocabulary in advance created anxiety. When unpredictable events turn out other than expected, a natural feeling of surprise is translated into an uncomfortable sense of confusion. Secondly, unrealistic objects and actions, such as painting a canvas without using actual paint, befuddles literal thinkers who expect all physical realities to be visualised on stage. When employing minimalist scenery, such as one large box to represent a home and a school, children may know when locales change by actors' movements but still feel annoyed when settings do not materially differentiate between separate fictional locations.

Thirdly, children often report confusion when they want to know particular reasons and underlying motivations for characters' surprising actions that remain unspecified. For example, why would Don Quixote return to his escapades a second time after failing the first? The dialogue in *This Is Not a Pipe Dream* does not tell why René Magritte's mother killed herself, how she died and why his father didn't want him be an artist. Leaving such curious questions unanswered leaves some children feeling dissatisfied until they recognise their responsibilities as imaginative interpreters by trusting their self-efficacious cognitive abilities.

Comparing theatre and television

To explore children's perceptions of a medium's cognitive demands, we asked 6, 8 and 11 year olds to compare media differences between theatre and television by asking the following questions: 'Would you rather go to see (play title) as a play on a stage like you did yesterday, or watch a production of it on television at home?' followed by 'What's the difference?' For the computer-animated version of *Dinosaurus*, we asked, 'Have you ever seen a movie, TV, or puppet show and/or played a video or computer game about dinosaurs?' and if so, 'How was this different from the play you saw yesterday?' During the late 1980s, a majority reported preferring theatre over television in a ratio of about three to one, primarily for its live qualities. Virtually identical media distinctions were reported in 2001. It appears that for each child who prefers television, three children prefer live theatre.

Those who prefer theatre rate their peers' enjoyment of productions significantly higher than those who prefer television, and they are also more likely to perceive an educational purpose to theatre, perhaps as a function of their school's field trip. As these viewers search for information relevant to their lives, they pay closer attention to visual and verbal cues and integrate these cues to make more metaphoric applications regarding play themes. This attention is significantly more than for those children who prefer to watch television as habitual viewers. These findings suggest that children perceive the greater cognitive demands of live theatre over commercial television programmes by investing sufficient mental effort (Klein, 2005:44-6).

Recalling the story and characters' actions and emotions

Following well-established procedures in the field of developmental psychology, the next set of questions are ordered from the most to least difficult to remember: from free story recall, to cued recall, to recognition tasks. Free story recall proves most advantageous for non-realistic plays structured episodically by situational relationships among three characters. To assist working memory, 6 and 7 year olds use character dolls, front and back photos of actors pasted on thin wood and small scenic reconstructions to re-dramatise the play's story. After clarifying the names of each character, we say, 'Let's pretend you have a friend who didn't see the play yesterday. Use these toys to show and tell your friend what happened in the play' or 'what the play was about'. This is prompted by, 'What else happened?' or 'What else was the play about?' Even when provided with such props, older children prefer to recall the play verbally 'to a friend who didn't see the play.' Inducing third-person perspectives encourages more elaborations than possibly skipping some information for the interviewer who has presumably seen the play.

Free story recall provides the most detailed data for analysing interpretations of episodic plot events or the causes and consequences of characters' central actions and incidental activities, as well as word choices. For example, in *Crying to Laugh*, surprisingly few children recalled that the play was about feelings or emotions, whilst older children were more likely to use emotion labels, behaviours and internal states to recount the story (Klein, 1995:56-7).

Plot-sequencing tasks offer another behavioural method for discerning visual and verbal memories of dramatised structures. Children aged 8 and up are assigned randomly to sequence the play in its proper chronological order, using cards which have either only photographed scenes or photographed scenes with pieces of scripted dialogue on the back. They use the same mixed array of five or seven central scenes and turn the cards over in their own time. Most children prefer to sequence scenes more quickly and efficiently by using photographs and reading dialogue only when needed to reinforce their recall of visualised actions. As predicted by mnemonic studies, beginnings and endings are recalled best, regardless of visual or verbal conditions, with middles more muddled, especially when episodic plays lack causal connections between scenes (eg. van den Broek, 1997:335).

Cued recall involves more specific questions, with or without photographed prompts, that require inferences concerning anything of pertinent interest to each study, such as recalling a play's main thematic ideas. We found that rather than asking, 'What do you think was the main idea or lesson of the play?' children offer a broader range of conceptual ideas when asked, 'What do you think (the protagonist) learned at the end of the play?' Responses for main ideas are coded from emergent categories ranging from abstract to concrete ideas. The majority of children interpret thematic concepts simply by recounting what characters did and said during performances, whilst a minority go beyond performance confines by abstracting themes about human conditions (Klein, 2005:50-2). Asking what a character meant when he or she said a line of dialogue that expresses a play's main idea offers another way of discovering whether intended ideas were communicated. For instance, when asked what René Magritte meant by 'If everything is possible, there are no pipe dreams', responses depended in part on whether children grasped the term 'pipe dream', as defined by the Interlocutor earlier in the performance (Klein, 1993:15).

Recognition tasks involve asking respondents to recognise particular images or abstract concepts and to choose from amongst multiple- or forced-choice responses. To gather inferences with regards to characters' emotions during particular situations, we prompt memories using photographs taken during dress rehearsals that depict long-shot views of the scene from where respondents sat with actors' faces blanked out so that children do not rely on photographed facial expressions to name emotions. We ask, 'When (this situation happened), how did (a character) feel?' by having children verbalise or point to respective schematic drawings of facial expressions labelled as happy, sad, mad, surprised, scared, disgusted, and OK or neutral as references. Using a graphically worded strip of paper, we then ask, 'Did (she or he) feel a little bit, or pretty, or VERY VERY (named emotion)?' or 'How much did (the character) feel that? A little or A LOT?' We then ask, 'How do you know (the character) felt that way?' or 'How did you decide (the character) felt (named emotion)? Was it something you saw, heard or felt?' and 'What did you see, hear or feel?'

Interpreting constructs of perceived reality and empathy

The multidimensional and interconnected constructs of perceived reality and empathy depend on how researchers interpret theories regarding willing suspensions of disbelief and aesthetic distance before wording specific questions and coding emergent categories. By age 4, young spectators know full well various distinctions between fantasy-reality and false beliefs. They also decide how metaphorically near or far they want to empathise with, sympathise for, and distance themselves from actors and characters in varying situations, based on subjective and objective stances that continually change during performances (Klein, 2005:48-50; Klein and Schonmann, 2009:68-71).

For the *Pipe Dream* study, when asked what was 'make-believe' or 'not real', 'actually real', or 'realistic' or 'seemed like it was real' in the play, responses reflected individuals' meanings of these words and the theatrical frames of the play-within-a-play production. Children did not necessarily suspend their disbelief willingly because the Interlocutor deluded audiences with numerous examples of theatrical reality and broke aesthetic distance by interrupting Magritte's story frequently; for instance, by stopping to define 'pipe dream' for spectators. Given these delusional framing conventions, children searched for and found illogical actions, inauthentic objects, fantastical characters and unbelievable events that countered their literal rules of physical and social reality (Klein, 1993:14; Klein and Schonmann, 2009:70-1).

In the *Dinosaurus* study, whether children labelled the computer-animated dinosaurs 'make-believe' or 'realistic', the majority projected human emotions onto the screen images within the play's fictional frame as artists intended. While most perceived the human dinosaur chorus as 'actually real' or 'realistic', they did not ascribe emotions to the actors until asked directly what these people felt. During the questioning, whilst many children noted character emotions from actors' behaviours within the fictional or representational frame, almost half focused on the actors' pretence within a theatrical or presentational context (Klein, 2003:43-4).

The *Crying to Laugh* study probed more deeply into constructs of empathy, sympathy, and distancing. Before asking how characters felt in each of six situations, we asked, 'How did you feel (when this situation happened)?' 'How much did you feel that?' and 'What made you feel that way?' After much discussion between myself and two interpreters, we defined and coded reported reasons for various emotions by three emergent categories from actors' subjective or spectators' objective perspectives and no attributions. Empathy is defined as identical matches with actors' subjective emotions and actor-characters' spoken reasons. Sympathy is defined as plausible emotions with objective reasons different from actor-characters' reasons.

Whilst empathy and sympathy refer to emotions reported within fictional or representational frameworks, distancing is defined as personal opinions made outside the fiction or inside a theatrical or presentational framework. Based on these definitions, most children sympathised and distanced themselves from objective perspectives, and half empathised from actors' subjective perspectives with several significant age and gender differences (Klein, 1995:55-62).

Vicarious identifications with characters also depend on whether spectators perceive actor-characters as first-person subjects or third-person objects of themselves. To gather such perspectives regarding specific characters, we ask, 'How much are you like (this character)? A little, a lot, or not at all?' and 'How are you (a little or a lot) like (this character)?' or 'How are you different from (this character)?' Six to 8 year olds tend to perceive similarities and differences objectively, on the basis of physical appearances and active or behavioural traits, whilst older children rely more on comparing characters' emotional, social and moral traits in relation to themselves from their subjective viewpoints (Klein, 2005:49-50).

Inferring artistic intentions for conventions

Artists may presume that children understand many taken-for-granted theatre conventions, such as onstage costume changes for doubled roles. However, asking children to interpret artists' intended meanings of various conventions may offer surprising reasoning. For the *Pipe Dream* study we posed several open-ended questions with photographed prompts regarding conventional expressions of various visual, verbal and kinesthetic metaphors. For instance, when asked, 'Why were Magritte's paintings or pictures projected on the screen during the whole play?' most children thought they were intended simply to show his artwork or to add general beauty, and fewer interpreted them as visualisations of René's imagination during specific moments in the performance (Klein, 1993:15-6). When asked why artists included both screen and human dinosaurs on stage in *Dinosaurus* and what difference it made, reasons reflected artists' intentions as well as children's own pragmatic speculations (Klein, 2003:44-5).

How do you know?

Asking, 'How do you know?' after each cued recall or recognition question evokes deeper, more critical and self-reflective awareness of knowing about knowing. Responses to this classic metacognitive question reveal not only what images children select for attention purposes but the primary sources of knowledge they rely upon most to encode, decode and recall dramatised stories. Multiple categories of metacognition from explicit and implicit sources within and outside productions emerge from coding all evidence. The following sources of evidence allow artists to know which perceptual and conceptual modes communicated intended ideas best.

Within productions, explicit images refer to semiotic categories used to analyse how performances generate and communicate meanings to spectators. Explicit visual images include what actor-characters do physically or their dramatised actions; how they act or their general acting behaviours, gestures and facial expressions; and their physical appearances, as well as the physical realism of costumes, props and scenic and lighting environments. Explicit verbal images include what actor-characters actually say and communicate in their dialogue and tones of voice, as well as sound effects and music. Psychological inferences refer to what actor-characters think and feel implicitly, or their unstated motives, thoughts, feelings, opinions, traits and sensory perceptions based on analyses of respective scripts that spectators must construct from available explicit cues. Outside production sources include general life knowledge about the world at large, theatre knowledge and expectations regarding dramatised stories and general performance factors, recollections of personal associations and children's abiding criteria regarding social realism.

In general, results from each study reveal that the more young spectators report using visual cues, primarily characters' dramatic actions, or, in the case of 6 year olds, the actors' behaviour, the more they also report using verbal-aural cues and making inferences about actors' internalised thoughts. The more they integrate available visual, verbal-aural and psychological cues, the more they report learning major thematic concepts in plays. Explicit dialogue concerning a protagonist's primary goal also increases opportunities for inferring abstract ideas about a play's theme.

Future challenges

While the evidence from these and other international studies may or may not surprise theatre researchers and artists, their findings affirm common cognitive-affective principles that developmental psychologists take for granted. Nevertheless, I hope that these recommended questioning and coding methods may assist UK researchers in their future reception studies, as well as theatre producers who seek to express their intended meanings with optimal success.

Given an accumulation of research discoveries from international reception studies over the past thirty years, it appears to me that the evidence from such studies has not made any discernible difference on the profession of theatre for young audiences. Whilst reception studies provide invaluable opportunities for children to reflect upon performances and deepen their critical appreciations, once researchers and artists know what, how and why they responded to particular productions as they did, artists and researchers seldom apply such discoveries to their future work in order to address and resolve ongoing and larger problems within and outside the profession.

From my vantage point in the United States, it appears to me that reception studies are treated as one-time past events that have little to no future impact upon the profession as a whole, much like ephemeral and localised performances themselves. I find that most theatre people believe fervently that the singular contexts of different child spectators and different theatre productions render respective aesthetic and artistic sides of the communication equation unique, unrepeatable and non-generaliseable to other contexts. For these reasons, artists tend to disregard evidence from reception studies, opting instead to reproduce theatrical traditions or create innovative experiments with as much risk-taking artistry as economic market conditions will allow.

For their part, many theatre researchers recreate reception studies primarily and simply by redefining theoretical and methodological constructs, unlike social science investigators who first conduct thorough literature reviews of past evidence in order to work on specific research questions that have yet to be answered. These investigators thereby build upon and change existing knowledge and practices.

Based on the evidence of my own and others' reception studies, I agree with Reason (2010:57) that inductive evidence does generalise to other child populations because the physiological nature and mediated nurturing of children's minds depends on the neurologically maturing properties of their malleable brains. Yet we need more deductive arguments that move from redefining general dramatic theories and reinterpreting embedded beliefs about children's competences to particular propositions that apply directly to artistic practices.

Rather than reproduce interpretations of children's interpretations of productions, researchers might synthesise and build upon the foundational evidence of children's emotion-driven minds across multiple, context-dependent reception studies to advance the profession's artistic knowledge. These deductive and critically reasoned challenges to existing inductive and multi-relative beliefs in current artistic practices require more emotionally resonant arguments and a mutual willingness to move beyond debilitating fears of losing faith in our respective epistemological positions (Klein, 2009:93-5). Yet by overcoming these understandable fears and inherently dramatic conflicts we may also conjoin a multiplicity of theories and practices and thereby establish more direct connections with all generational aesthetic experiences to prove why theatre spectatorship matters to global cultures.

References

Bennett, S (ed) (2005) *Theatre for Children and Young People: 50 years of professional theatre in the UK.* London: Aurora Metro Press

Deldime, R and Pigeon, J (1988) *La Memoire du Jeune Spectateur.* Bruxelles: De Boeck-Wesmael

Klein, J (1987) Children's processing of theatre as a function of verbal and visual recall. *Youth Theatre Journal* 2(1) p9-13

Klein, J (1993) Applying research to artistic practices: This Is Not a Pipe Dream. *Youth Theatre Journal* 7(3) p13-17

Klein, J (1995) Performance factors that inhibit empathy and trigger distancing: Crying to Laugh. *Youth Theatre Journal* 9 p53-67

Klein, J (2003) Children's interpretations of computer-animated dinosaurs in theatre. *Youth Theatre Journal* 17 p38-50

Klein, J (2005) From children's perspectives: a model of aesthetic processing in theatre. *Journal of Aesthetic Education* 39(4) p40-57

Klein, J (2009) Mapping aesthetic development and epistemological understanding. *Journal of Dramatic Theory and Criticism* 24(1) p83-97

Klein, J (2010) Mediating childhood: how child spectators interpret actors' bodies in theatrical media. In Lipscomb, VB and Marshall, L (eds) *Staging Age: the performance of age in theatre, dance, and film.* New York: Palgrave Macmillan

Klein, J and Fitch, M (1989) Third grade children's verbal and visual recall of Monkey, Monkey. *Youth Theatre Journal* 4(2) p9-15

Klein, J and Fitch, M (1990) First grade children's comprehension of Noodle Doodle Box. *Youth Theatre Journal* 5(2) p7-13

Klein, J and Schonmann, S (2009) Theorizing aesthetic transactions from children's criterial values in theatre for young audiences. *Youth Theatre Journal* 23(1) p60-74

Kuhn, D (2011) What is scientific thinking and how does it develop? In Goswami, U (ed) *The Wiley-Blackwell Handbook of Childhood Cognitive Development.* West Sussex: Wiley-Blackwell

Reason, M (2010) *The Young Audience: exploring and enhancing children's experiences of theatre.* Stoke on Trent: Trentham

Saldaña, J (1996) 'Significant differences' in child audience response: assertions from the ASU longitudinal study. *Youth Theatre Journal* 10 p67-83

Schonmann, S (2006) *Theatre as a Medium for Children and Young People: images and observations.* Dordrecht, Springer

van den Broek, P (1997) Discovering the cement of the universe: the development of event comprehension from childhood to adulthood. In van den Broek, P W, Bauer, P J and Bourg, T (eds) *Developmental Spans in Event Comprehension and Representation: bridging fictional and actual events.* Mahwah, NJ: Erlbaum

Winston, J (2003) Playing on The Magic Mountain: theatre education and teaching training at a children's theatre in Brussels. *Research in Drama Education* 8(2) p203-16

Notes on contributors

Gill Brigg is a theatre writer, director and teacher. She comes from an educational background, having worked in all phases of education as a drama teacher and advisory teacher undertaking an MEd by research at The Cambridge Institute of Education. Her freelance career has increasingly focused on creating theatre for audiences labelled as having profound and multiple learning disabilities, touring one woman shows as a performer over a ten year period and receiving commissions from the Wolsey Theatre, Ipswich and Nottingham Playhouse. Gill has presented papers at the University of Westminster and University of Nottingham. She is a guest lecturer within the English Studies department at the University of Nottingham and works with students of theatre design at Nottingham Trent University. Gill sits on the TYA UK planning committee for disability arts and is on the Board of Directors for both Eastern Angles and Bamboozle Theatre Company.

David Broster spent a significant part of his professional theatre life in the area of theatre for young people where he worked as an actor, actor/teacher, writer and director with a number of established companies in the field. He moved into the university sector as a lecturer in the mid 1990's and is currently Head of Drama, Performance and Film at the University of Worcester, where he teaches on the BA Drama and Performance course and MA Drama: Theatre and Young People. In 2005 he established the Magic Attic Theatre Company, which operates from the university, with the aim of producing new work and engaging with research into young audiences' responses to the theatre experience. As a member of the International Theatre for Young Audiences Research Network (ITYARN) he has spoken at international conferences and written on subjects such as TYA, culture and society, taboos and the parameters of theatre for young audiences.

Dominic Hingorani is an academic, writer and professional theatre director. He is a senior lecturer in the School of Arts and Digital Industries at the University of East London and Programme Leader of the MA Acting and MA Theatre Directing. Dominic has written widely on British Asian Theatre including a monograph *British*

Asian Theatre – Dramaturgy Process and Performance (2010) published by Palgrave Macmillan. He is currently under commission to write *Theatre For Young Audiences: Contemporary Approaches to Practice and Performance*. Dominic is co-artistic director of Brolly Productions, a company that creates projects across art forms and promotes interdisciplinary collaborations for whom he has recently created and directed a stage adaptation of *Guantanamo Boy* by Anna Perera which will tour nationally in 2013. Dominic originally trained at the Royal Scottish Academy of Music and Drama and worked as a professional actor in theatre, film, television and on radio.

Jeanne Klein is an associated professor of theatre at the University of Kansas (USA) where she has directed over twenty productions for child audiences. She teaches theatre for young audiences, drama with children and child media psychology courses, as well as US theatre history. Her nationally award-winning reception studies and theoretical models of spectatorship have been published in the *Youth Theatre Journal, Theatre Research in Canada, Canadian Children's Literature, Journal of Aesthetic Education*, and *Journal of Dramatic Theory and Criticism*. She has attended various international TYA festivals and ASSITEJ Congresses in Australia, Canada, Denmark, France, Japan, the Netherlands, Sweden and the United States.

Tom Maguire is a senior lecturer in Theatre Studies at the School of Creative Arts of the University of Ulster. He teaches and researches in the areas of contemporary British and Irish theatre, theatre for young audiences, applied theatre and storytelling. He has published extensively on theatre in Northern Ireland. He has written, directed and performed in productions for children for over fifteen years. Since 2009, he has collaborated with Young at Art to curate the Making Space symposium as part of the Belfast Children's Festival. He is a member of the Editorial Board for *About Performance* and Chair of the Board of Big Telly Theatre Company, Northern Ireland. He is a freelance theatre critic contributing to *Irish Theatre Magazine* and BBC Radio Ulster's Arts Extra.

Geoff Readman has worked extensively in drama and theatre, as teacher, director, actor-teacher, county drama inspector and university lecturer for over forty years. He taught in both primary and secondary schools before leading Wakefield DiE Team for eight years. In 1983 he became County Inspector for Drama in Nottinghamshire, which was followed by appointment to Bishop Grosseteste University College, where he introduced a degree in community theatre. From 1998 to 2004, he was Head of Drama at Island School, Hong Kong, a post he combined with lecturing at Hong Kong University, where he became Visiting Professor of Drama. His recent work has included directing TiE with 'Language Alive!' in Birmingham and his current PhD research, which is registered with the University of Northampton, is examining the contribution of the director in applied theatre contexts.

Matthew Reason is Reader in Theatre and Head of Programme for MA Studies in Creative Practice at York St John University. His research explores the experiential qualities of art and he has published on themes relating to performance documentation, reflective practice, audience research, theatre for young audiences, contemporary performance and cultural policy. He has written two books: *Documentation, Disappearance and the Representation of Live Performance* (Palgrave, 2006) and *The Young Audience: Exploring and Enhancing Children's Experiences of Theatre* (Trentham, 2010). Between 2008-11 he worked on the 'Watching Dance: Kinesthetic Empathy' project (www.watchingdance.org) and has recently edited, with Dee Reynolds, Kinesthetic Empathy in Creative and Cultural Contexts (Intellect, 2012).

James Reynolds is a lecturer in Drama at Kingston University. His PhD research at Queen Mary, University of London, investigated performance practices in Robert Lepage's devised theatre. Published work includes studies of Howard Barker's direction of his own plays (*Theatre of Catastrophe*, 2006); Lepage's work with objects (*Performance Research*, 2007); and the cinematic adaptation of graphic novels (*Journal of Adaptation in Film and Performance*, 2009). He has also published on applied theatre work in the field of recovery from addiction in *The Journal of Applied Arts and Health* (2011).

Karian Schuitema's doctoral research project concerned children's theatre in the UK and the representation of cultural diversity, focusing on aspects of interculturalism, multiculturalism and internationalism. She has created the Children's Theatre in the UK Research Network and organised a conference on the subject of theatre for the young at the University of Westminster. Her publications include: 'The Possibility of an Intercultural Children's Theatre in Britain' in *The Sands of Time, Children's Literature: Culture, Politics and Identity*, edited by Jenny Plastow and Margot Hillel (University of Hertfordshire Press, 2010); and 'Staging and Performing *His Dark Materials*: From the National Theatre Productions to Subsequent Productions' in *Critical Perspectives on Philip Pullman's His Dark Materials*, edited by Steve Barfield and Katherine Cox (McFarland and company, 2011).

Tim Webb is a co-founder of the Oily Cart and over the past thirty years has written and directed over seventy shows for the company. The company creates work for two audiences: very young children (6 months to 6 years old) and young people with Profound and Multiple Learning Disability and/or an Autistic Spectrum Disorder aged 3-19. He is on the board of TYA-England and Ockham's Razor and was appointed MBE in 2011 for services to drama for children with special needs. His scripts have been produced at the Leicester Haymarket, the Albany Empire, Contact Theatre, Manchester, and by Greenwich, Glasgow and Leeds Theatre-in-Education companies. Tim has directed productions for, amongst others, the Lyric Theatre, Belfast, the London Bubble, Canada's Carousel Players and the Chicago Children's Theatre.

David Wood OBE is called 'the national children's dramatist' (The Times). For twenty five years he directed his own plays for his company, Whirligig Theatre, that toured major UK theatres. His plays are performed worldwide and include *The Gingerbread Man, The Plotters of Cabbage Patch Corner, Save the Human* and *The Ideal Gnome Expedition.* Among his adaptations are eight Roald Dahl stories, Eric Hill's *Spot's Birthday Party,* HRH the Prince of Wales' *The Old Man of Lochnagar,* Philip Pullman's *Clockwork,* Judith Kerr's *The Tiger Who Came to Tea,* Sam McBratney's *Guess How Much I Love You,* Michelle Magorian's *Goodnight Mister Tom* and the award-winning *Tom's Midnight Garden* (from Philippa Pearce's novel). For the Queen's 80th birthday, he wrote *The Queen's Handbag,* broadcast live from Buckingham Palace Gardens to 8,000,000 BBC1 viewers. He is the Chair of Action for Children's Arts. Visit his website at www.davidwood.org.uk.

Jan Wozniak is a postgraduate research student at Queen Mary, University of London, where he is researching contemporary theatrical production and the reception of Shakespeare for young people. He is interested in the cultural politics of performance as it emerges both at the moment of performance and in performance traces. Jan is particularly interested in working with young people to research their own experience of performance and on exploring with them a variety of approaches to documenting and responding to performance.

Peter Wynne-Willson is a writer and director of theatre for young audiences, based in Birmingham. From 1982-92 he was the founding artistic director of Big Brum Theatre-in-Education Company, where he initially worked within a devising team, before concentrating more on writing. He has written forty plays including *The Broken Peace* for Greenwich YPT, *Saving Hope* for Language Alive, *Roy, Homeland* and *Heads or Tails* for Big Brum, and *The Shooky* and *Princess and Ginger* for Birmingham Rep. From 1999-2005 he was Visiting Professor of Theatre-in-Education at the Korean National University of the Arts in Seoul. The association with Korea has led to seven new plays, including bilingual plays The Bridge in 2005 (revived for ASSITEJ World Congress in Adelaide in 2008) and, most recently, *Looking for Yoghurt.* In recent years he has been increasingly involved in early years work, as a key artist and story-maker in the 'Moonbeams' research projects.

Index